The Revolutionary Subhash

Dr. Giriraj Sharan Agrawal

DIAMOND BOOKS

© Author

Publisher : **Diamond Pocket Books (P) Ltd.**
X-30, Okhla Industrial Area, Phase-II
New Delhi-110020
Phone : 011-40712200
E-mail : sales@dpb.in
Website : www.diamondbook.in

The Revolutionary Subhash
By - *Dr. Giriraj Sharan Agrawal*

PART – I

Chapter - 1

The young boy was engrossed in his studies in his study room. He was unaware that his father Jankidas Bose had come to his room to say something to him but returned back after standing behind him for some time. His mother Prabhadevi had been standing behind him for quite long with Goddess Durga's *prasada* (offering made for goddesses).

"Son, take this *prasada* of Goddess Durga." One address was not enough to break the boy's silence. The mother again asked, "Son, what are you studying in such an engrossed manner? For how long I have to stand here? Take this offering made to Goddess Durga." Saying this, the mother kept the *prasada* in front of Subhash.

The boy stood up. The mother saw a drastic change in son's behavior.

"Mother, will this *prasada* help me to gain strength and power from goddess Durga?"

"Son, mother Durga is the strength. Whatever you offer with complete devotion becomes the abode of that goddess. You should not show aversion to it."

"Mother, you have told me many times that Goddess Durga is the epitome of strength. Strength should be worshipped with strength itself. Offering flowers and sweets would be like insulting Her."

"Son, what happened to you? What changes have taken place in you? Who has been influencing you?"

"Mother, today our country is in dire need of sacrifices. This idol of the goddess holding these weapons giving us this indication. Now we should not worship Her with fruits, flowers and sweets but with weapons."

Subhash's face reddened, he took out a knife from his table, slit his finger and marked a '*tilak*' on the forehead of the picture of Goddess Durga hanging in front of his table.

The mother stood stunned and speechless.

Chapter - 2

"The cruel laws of British government have taken us to the brink of poverty and helplessness. Babuji, we should break the shackles of dependence at any cost. Now we should do something or the other to attain freedom."

"But Subhash, at this young age, in spite of you enthusiasm, what can you do?"

"Babuji, I can sacrifice my life to expel The British from our country. But I cannot bear their presence in our country anymore."

Babu Veni Madhav was utterly stunned by the enthusiasm and excitement of young Subhash Chandra Bose. Babu Veni Madhav was the Principal of Collegiate High School. He was a very kind person and a true patriot. He was the actual source of inspiration for Subhash Chandra Bose. Subhash always approached Babuji to clarify any doubt that came to his mind at any point of time. Babu Veni Madhav was well aware of Subhash's qualities and he readily listened to Subhash and answered his questions, even at times when he was busy.

Today when Subhash came to him, he was entangled in a major problem relating to the school. If it had been any one else other than Subhash, he would have definitely avoided him. But Subhash's very presence enthralled him and gave him pleasure. He forgot his own problems and began to talk with Subhash, although he had not been able to read the newspaper of the day.

"Subhash, I am really happy with your revolutionary thoughts, but at the same time I am really worried about you. How will you be able to give your thoughts a concrete shape?"

"Babuji, I feel you also have your doubts about me. Is it not the responsibility of every citizen of this country to break the shackles of foreign rule? Is it so that the blood running in our veins have gone dry? Has it become bereft of passion and heat?"

Babu Veni Madhav became anxious. He said, "No Subhash, this is not the matter. The British are in no mood to loosen their reins on this country. They do not want anyone causing trouble to their peaceful life. They will not be reluctant to take the strongest action possible to repress any such uprising. At that time they won't differentiate between legality and illegality."

A storm of decision and indecision was going on in the mind of Subhash. He was not as much anxious about his future as he was about the present condition of the country, its poverty, the step motherly treatment of Indians by Britishers. The shine on his face reflected his ambition, his curiosity and his excitement.

After a short silence Subhash said, "Babuji. Is the British government taking a correct legal stance, that it will do justice to our revolutions? In the eyes of Britishers, we Indians are not human beings. The condition of Indians is worse than that of wild animals. They have no life supporting system. The government is least bothered whether they are alive or dead. Perhaps you have not read today's newspaper till now—Jajpur is in the grip of deadly *cholera* which is spreading like wildfire affecting thousands of people. Innumerable people have died of it and the government is doing nothing. Now, you tell me, how can we remain calm in such a situation? Should we let our countrymen die like cattle? Don't we have any responsibilities towards them?"

These questions of Subhash silenced Babu Veni Madhav. Anxiety was clearly evident on his forehead. He took the newspaper lying in front of him and began reading it. Tears came rolling out from his eyes. He said, "Your concern is natural. Every rational person is tormented by the condition of the country, but what can we do in such a difficult situation?"

"Babuji, we are clear about our duties. We should put in every effort to break the shackles of our mother India which is on the brink of death and starvation. Thousands of people are dying in Jajpur and the government is sitting idle without doing anything. This is the heights of their injustice. How long can we bear this torment?"

"Subhash, you know very well that opposing British rule is a futile attempt."

"I know Babuji, but power could be subdued by power only. I will be instrumental in constructing that power that will fight our enemy as well as our country's poverty. I want to build such a power and awareness in the minds of our countrymen that will prove to be a source of inspiration to them till the end."

"But you alone…."

"Babuji…."

Subhash was compelled to interrupt Babu Veni Madhav's words. A fire was burning in his heart. Images of poverty and illness were flipping before his mind's eye. He said in an enthusiastic tone, "Babuji, I know what you are going to say that, at this moment, I am alone and small. But nothing can happen by sitting idly and peacefully. We should continue with our efforts, each and every moment."

"You are right, Subhash. Taking efforts is essential. Your duty is also clear. Whatever path you choose, you should be clear about your objectives."

"If it is so, then our duty is to save our fellow countrymen. Something should be done to save the lives of residents of Jajpur. I am leaving for Jaipur without any delay."

"Why?" Veni Madhav asked in surprise.

"I have to save the lives of the inhabitants of Jajpur."

"Subhash, I am not able to understand how you are going to face this communicable disease. My advice to you is not to go there. I am afraid that......"

"Babuji, I will go there at any cost. It is my firm decision."Babu Veni Madhav knew very well that once Subhash takes any resolution he never backs out from it. Hence he was compelled to leave him to his decision."

"Then I will also accompany you, Subhash. This way I will be able to utilize my holidays in a worthwhile manner. Go and make arrangements for it."

Chapter - 3

For two months both the teacher and the student helped the poor and hapless people. What they witnessed all around was the pathetic condition of people struck by disease and starvation.

Subhash returned back home after two months serving and taking care of the diseased and the hungry. He went straight to his father's room. Seeing his son standing in front of him after such a long time, father Jankidas shrieked with happiness.

Subhash had become very weak due to restless service of the cholera patients. Seeing the condition of their son, both the father's and mother's eyes swelled up with tears. His father somehow controlled his emotions and said "Subhash!"

"Yes, father......"

"Where have you gone without informing us? Do good boys do such things? Are you not concerned about your health?"

"Jajpur," Subhash gave a short answer and stood silent.

"Jajpur!" father exclaimed in surprise. "There is an outbreak of dangerous cholera over there, why did you go there?"

"I had to serve the people there. When I heard that people

are dying there I could not restrain myself. I was keen to help those poor and hapless."

"But Subhash, don't you know cholera is a communicable disease?"

"I know."

"Even then you went there? Are you not concerned about yourself?"

"Father, as you are concerned about me, think of the residents of Jajpur who were in a helpless condition, witnessing the deaths of their children being unable to give them proper treatment. I went to help them out in such a condition."

"O.K. you went there to serve them? Son of Rai Bahadur Janakidas, who has in his home a dozen servants to serve him, had gone to serve the poor and helpless. Are you not a bit concerned about my status?" Jankidas asked in changed tone.

Subhash was silent.

"You have chosen the profession of serving them like a person of lowly birth. And you forgot that you are the son of that Rai Bahadur who is being honored by high ranking officers even."

Suddenly, Subhash's facial expression changed. He broke his silence and said, "Father, I don't think that my act of serving those people has in any way affected your status. In fact, I have enhanced your honor by saving people from the brink of death. Those parents, the lives of whose children have been saved by me, must have given me blessing. When they used to say that the parents to whom I am born are really lucky ones, I used to feel really proud."

Before Janakidas could say anything further or Subhash could make any more revolutionary statements, his mother Prabhadevi took her son, Subhash, away.

"You have become so skinny. You might not have got proper food even. Come, have something to eat."

Chapter - 4

'Life is like a spring balance, where both truth and untruth gets weighed. And it is general human tendency that sometimes they give emphasis to truth and sometimes to untruth. Those people, who in spite of all hardships of life do not let untruth weigh upon them, are the ones who have led a meaningful life. Whereas those who live in falsehood are devoid of life. Hence to enjoy life in its real sense, search for truth.' These words by Swami Dayanand kept on reverberating in the ears of Subhash.

An intense emotion came over him, 'Search for truth.' He had been a thinker since childhood. He had passed his high school only a few days ago and had got admission in the Presidency College. There he didn't feel comfortable when he saw boys belonging to rich families wasting money in restaurant and hotels. Images of people dying of hunger and disease always reflected in his mind's eye. But how can he say anything to others. To convince himself was not easier for him. So he kept himself aloof from such company and declined any invitation to such places. He spent his time in philosophical thoughts and finding out solutions for the current problems of the country.

He always used to think that we ourselves are responsible for the present condition of our country and we have the power to act according to our will. If the present condition is the result of our past action, we can be instrumental in securing a good future by means of present action. Sometimes he used to think that human beings will become real human beings only if they constantly strive to outgrow nature. Slowly his mind and heart became influenced by spirituality.

His interest towards his college lessons began to decrease. Swami Vivekanand's philosophical thinking made a deep impact on him. The revolutionary thoughts in his mind broke all the bounds and barriers. He was unable to decide as to which path he should choose to search for truth. He read the stories about different saints who had chosen this path and made a soul searching in every aspect. The only way left was to take shelter under any of the Himalayan caves in search for truth. He transformed his decision into reality by leaving his home without informing anyone.

Darkness pervaded the night but his mind was all inclined and inspired to search for light and truth. He kept on walking crossing caves, jungles and ashrams of saints and holy men. But he could not find even a glance of truth anywhere. Days passed by but he could not find truth. Everywhere the environment was full of hatred and sinfulness and he could not bear to stand at such places even for a while.

He could get no peace of mind in the lonely mountains of the Himalayas. There also worldliness and unrest prevailed. Fed up of that place he went to Mathura. There he met Swami Parmanand. Swamiji was a graduate but his life style was that of a family man. Subhash didn't like all this and he left the place.

From Mathura, Subhash went to Vrindavan. One saint Ramkrishnadas was greatly influenced and impressed by the personality of Subhash. He advised Subhash to go to Varanasi for further research and studies.

Subhash left for Varanasi. For many days he discussed with Swami Brahmanand of Ramakrishna Mission regarding his intention. But Swamiji did not want this young and intelligent boy to take up *sanyasa* without the permission of his parents. At last he asked Subhash to return back to his home.

Subhash readily accepted Swamiji's order and left Kashi for his home. But he was unhappy that he was not able to fulfill the objective with which he left his home. He was not able to have even a glance of truth during in his search.

Chapter - 5

Mother's worries kept on increasing. Other family members were unable to pacify her or even witness her sorrowful countenance. Father Janakidas' heart also cried but he showed outward strength and pacified his wife with encouraging words. He had made up his mind that whatever was destined will take place.

They had send letters to many of their friends and relatives.

Somebody advised him to inform the police. But one of his relatives who himself was a Police officer discouraged him from doing so.

There was no news regarding Subhash's well-being from anywhere. Prabha Devi's condition deteriorated and she behaved like an insane woman.

Everyone felt helpless as to what to do and what not to do.

At last, Subhash's maternal uncle was sent in search of Subhash. He searched for Subhash at Vaidyanath Dham (Devghar) but in vain. Their worries kept on increasing day by day.

Search for Subhash now began to be conducted at Belur. A telegraph was sent to Ramkrishna Mission situated in Haridwar. But no response was received. Now a letter came from Subhash's maternal uncle. He had written that- "I had gone to Balanandji. There one Brahmachari had told me that if Subhash has embraced sanyasa unofficially he will return back after many hassles. And if he is really eligible for sanyasa all efforts to make him return back home will be futile."

He also wrote that our astrologer had also told that Subhash will not be able to embrace sanyasa due to the effects of the country.

But the sorrows of his parents did not decrease. Her mother's eyes were swollen due to constant crying. Father's sorrows also knew no bounds. Who can measure the sorrow of the parents whose son has left the home without saying anything to anyone?

As the sorrows of both his father and other kept on increasing due to the emotions of love and affection that much of despair Subhash was experiencing as he came in contact with great saints. Wandering in the realm of unfulfilled hopes and indecisiveness, Subhash was not able to see any sign of fulfillment of his objective. His heart became overwhelmed to see the snobbery and affectation of the saints. How can they achieve spiritual peace? One cannot find out truth even in his dreams.

Subhash could not stand all these images of falsehood and returned back to Calcutta. The news of Subhash's return spread like wildfire and the whole house experienced turbulence.

The mother came running to her son and wept embracing her son. Seeing her son in front of her all her grief began to flow in the form of tears. She only said- "Have you born to kill me? I could not have survived so long. I would have ended my life jumping into the Ganga. But I could not do so thinking of my daughters."

Rai Bahadur Janakidas also came. He noticed he deteriorated health of his son and Subhash in turn glanced at him. Seeing his father's worried and pensive face, tears came to Subhash's eyes. Father embraced the long missing son.

He then took Subhash to his room. His countenance was serious.

"Subhash, look up at me!"

And, for a second, Subhash looked towards his father.

Tears trembled in his father's eyes. Seeing the tears in his father's eyes, the sorrow he experienced was equivalent to the sorrow the father had experienced when the son left home and even more when the son returned back.

"I wanted to find out truth. If I had sought your permission for it, you would not have given me the permission. Hence I left home without informing anyone."

"At least you could have sent a letter. Can you imagine how much worried we were? Have we become stranger in your eyes?"

Rai Bahadur Janakidas' tone sounded so miserable that Subhash could give no answer.

"You must have met some famous scholars and saints. Can you answer some of my questions which I am going to put across to you? First tell me, is there any religion in his world or not?"

"There is only one religion in this world and that is the religion of humanity."

"Is it possible to follow any religion as to live in the universe?"

"Every diseased person could not be healed with the help of a single medicine, because the strength varies from person to person and all are not victims of the same disease."

"Does sacrifice require meditation?"

"The concept of sacrifice depends on the cultural affinity of an individual. Everyone need not undergo a harsh kind of meditation because the power of endurance varies from person to person."

Subhash kept on answering and Janakidas listened in a state of shock. Then he asked— "Is it right to denounce one's duty?"

"In fact, duty is a conditional word. Actually to obey the orders of the elders is considered to be the duty of the younger ones. But after spiritual initiation, worldly relations and associated duties are left behind."

"Hun!" saying so Janakidas began to think something. "Subhash, the *Advaita* thinking of *Brahma* as the truth and the world a falsehood is just a philosophy or is it true?"

The answer to this question was wandering before his mind's eye in the most tangible form. His answer was full of simplicity, "As long as it is being pronounced with the mouth, it is a philosophy but after experiencing, it looks like a reality."

Father Janakidas felt happy hearing Subhash's arguments. He asked, "Are these your own thoughts or that of your Guru's?"

"Father, this is not the outcome of a single person's intellect or knowledge. It is the outcome of the experiences of those saints and scholars who have undergone this ecstasy. By following the path followed by them we can also achieve that unattainable object."

"Who is your ideal for all this?" The father asked his last question.

"Ram Krishna Paramhansa had proved all his and done all this." Subhash said, "Swami Vivekananda is my ideal."

Rai Bahadur could not say anything further.

Chapter - 6

This journey had completely shattered his bodily strength. His soft heart was hurt by his experiences during the journey. Whenever the image of the country's misery flashed before his mind's eye, tears came rolling down his cheeks.

Worry is a cause of sorrow for everyone. Subhash soon came under the attack of grave illness. Fever weakened his body.

His parents were all the more worried. But the efforts of the doctors resulted in the gradual recovery of Subhash's health. His will power also played a significant role in the improvement of his health.

No sooner than he recovered from his illness, his exams began. He prepared for his exam very well and completed his course in a short span of time.

Everyone was surprised when the result came. Subhash has passed the FA exam in first class. This was in the year 1915. Eighteen year old Subhash took admission in B.A. (Honors). His favorite subject was philosophy.

Chapter - 7

January 1916

Subhash reached the college library very early in the morning.

Suddenly there was turbulence in the library. Subhash get

distracted. He turned his eyes to see what was happening. He found some of his class mates along with Prof. E.F. Auten.

Prof. Auten was a hard core British. He had an attractive personality and fair complexion but while talking to his students he used the most unrefined language. That day also he was behaving with some students in rough manner.

Subhash could not tolerate cruelty and injustice. He came out form the library. Prof. Auten was threatening his students using foul languages. Before that he pushed some students standing in the lobby. Their crime was that they were standing in front of the professor's room in the verandah. And he began to call them 'wild uncivilized black Indians.'

Subhash could not bear this disgrace. He was the representative of his class and how could he bear such a cruelty meted out to class mates.

He instantly went to the principal and presented the matter before him. He said, "Sir, don't we Indian students have our existence? Are we not the students of this institute? A Professor, who should have showered his love and care on us are raining foul words on us. Since Prof. Auten has insulted us, he should seek forgiveness from the students."

But instead of pacifying and calming down the students, the Principal also behaved in a rude manner saying, "Mr. Auten has not insulted or behaved badly with any student nor has he used force against any student. He won't seek forgiveness from any one."

The students became agitated. The next day the students called a strike. The college authorities tried to influence the Muslim students and keep them away from the strike. But any kind of pressure on the part of the authorities could not have the desired impact. Nobody was successful in ending the agitation.

The success of the strike had its impact not only in Calcutta but it inspired the whole of India. Subhash was the leader of the striking students and was the cause of concern for the authorities.

Now the authorities began to put pressure on Mr. Auten. He was asked to solve the matter in consultation with the students' representatives. After much efforts and mutual discussion it was decided that the students would call off the strike and both the parties would arrive at an agreeable solution.

The strike ended but tension prevailed. One day, it was Prof. Auten's period. While teaching he made one student stand up and asked him many questions. He could not give any satisfactory answer because he could not understand the questions properly.

This was enough to flare up the anger of Prof. Auten. He shrieked at the student, "You stupid fellow. You do not concentrate on your studies and do not answer to my questions properly."

The student was least affected by such an address but Subhash was shocked.

The student answered, "Sir, I have not properly understood the question. Please make me understand again."

"You black monkey. You cannot even understand the question?"Suddenly Subhash stood up.

"Professor Sir, you are a civilized person. You should not use such uncivilized words. It does not sound nice from your mouth," Subhash said in a self-controlled humility.

"You bloody!" Professor shouted loudly, "Are you sitting on your seat or not?"

The use of foul language by the professor instigated him. He sprang forward and reached near the professor.

"What do you think of yourself professor? How dare you call such names? I will pull your tongue out."

And the very next moment, the imprint of Subhash's strong fingers was clearly marked on the Professor's fair countenance.

The incidence raised a huge uproar in the college. A British Professor being insulted by an Indian student. It was not a petty issue to be ignored considering insignificant. It was a great challenge to the college authority.

Today for the first time the Indians realized the importance of self-respect. For the first time, today they realized their existence. The flame of revolution instilled their mind. A feeling of hatred took birth in the minds of Indians towards the white people. Today it became evident that when a peaceful volcano erupts nobody can stand its dangerous flames.

This was the first time that a British was punished for his offensive behavior. British officer were taken aback by this revolt. They also believed that the behavior of the professor was improper. But they could not tolerate the act of the professor being slapped by a black and a slave.

The very next day Subhash was called by the Principal.

Subhash reached the room of the Principal at the scheduled time.

"Subhash, you are held responsible for creating problems in the college, hence you are rusticated from the college. You can no more continue with your studies," the Principal told him in a serious tone.

"Thank you!" Subhash also gave a brief answer.

After being expelled from the college, Subhash went to Cuttack where his father Rai Bahadur was at that time. He was surprised to find Subhash in front of him without any prior information. He said, "Oh, Subhash! What happened? What made you come here suddenly?"

Subhash related the whole incident that occurred in his college. He also informed his father that he has been expelled from the college.

"Subhash, you do not understand your responsibilities. By doing such an act you have spoilt your future. Are you aware that I have certain ambitions and expectations regarding you?"

"Father, in this kind of situation everyone thinks so. But you will come to know what future has in store for us after some days. Whatever I have done is exactly correct as far as I am concerned."

"You should not have come into any confrontation with

your professor," Rai Bahadur expressed his opinion in a serious tone.

"I had no intention of entering into a confrontation or conflict with the professor, but he insulted all the Indians. The foul words with which he addressed the students were not only an insult for us but for the whole of us. He should have got the punishment for that."

"But Subhash, you see, who got punished. Whatever be the case, you should not have taken up a fight for the sake of others. I have to say only this much."

"Father I live in this society and my friends are also a part of this society. The insult of any one of my friends is an insult for me. When the white British called my friend names and insulted him, I could not tolerate that."

"I am not able to understand the flow of your life."

Subhash had become very serious. After a gap of two seconds, as if immersed in serious thoughts he replied, "Father, the direction of my life will be formed by gaining India's independence and sacrificing my life for that. To attain freedom we need to sacrifice the lives of lakhs of young people."

Rai Bahadur Janakidas could not speak anything more.

Chapter - 8

March 1916

One month had lapsed since his expulsion from college. He was happy to see that there was no change in the behavior of his parents, brothers and other family members towards him. His relations with friends had become even more cordial and strong.

There was one big problem that Subhash had been facing— How to utilize the free time?

Studies had discontinued. There was no idea as to where he will get admission. He had been expelled from college for an indefinite period. He had kept all his books aside.

There was only one way open before Subhash to do social work. That was the only way where his mind and heart could have worked together in synchronized manner.

During those days there was an outbreak of cholera in Orissa. After reading the situation in Orissa from newspapers he used to feel very sad and depressed.

His duty consciousness awoke. He assembled his old friends and briefed them— "Friends, the effects of Cholera is spreading like wild fire. We all know that our poor fellow countrymen are suffering so much of hardships. They are not very capable of getting themselves treated by a doctor. We should help them out. We should seek the help of some of our sisters who will serve as nurses."

All his friends were greatly influenced by his words. It seemed like a magical spell.

Every arrangement was made in a few days.

Subhash worked day in and day out to make very sort of arrangement so as to ensure proper treatment of the patients.

First of all their team took charge of the cholera ward in Cuttack Civil Hospital. There were no trained nurses in the ward. The work was carried out by the untidy sweepers.

They found that the effect of cholera was more rampant in villages as compared to cities. They were so engrossed in serving the patients that they sometimes forgot about themselves. This way they saved the lives of many poor patients. They were so poor that sometimes their relatives were unable to bear the expenses of even their last rites. Subhash and his team took over this responsibility also on their shoulders. They collected money and helped such people. Sometimes they performed the last rites of orphaned dead bodies.

By the time the gravity of cholera somewhat educed and they were relieved from their social work, Subhash began to be haunted by the thoughts of his studies. One day he approached his father and said— "Father, I want to complete my studies. How can I do that? I would not get admission anywhere here. Can I not get admission in any foreign university?"

His father replied in a contemplative tone, "Subhash, I myself worried about you. I can send you abroad for further studies but I want to relieve you from defamation. My desire is that first you gain your degree from Calcutta University. You should send an application to the university requesting for the same."

Subhash, after receiving the blessings of his father went to Calcutta from Cuttack. He wanted to resolve the problem after discussion with the college authorities.

The job was not that easy. The decision was pending with Sir Ashutosh Mukherjee. He had played a major role in establishing the Calcutta University. Everything was in his hands and his one nod was enough to cancel the orders of his expulsion from college.

Year 1917

Subhash's happiness knew no bounds when he came to know that Calcutta University has cancelled its earlier orders and now he can get admission in any of the colleges affiliated to Delhi University.

One morning Subhash went and met the Principal of Scottish Church College and said, "I am a student being expelled from Presidency College but now the university has revoked its orders. I want to seek admission in B.A. (Philosophy) course in your college."

The Principal was impressed and happy with the personality of Subhash. He listened to Subhash patiently and with complete sympathy.

He said, "Subhash I am happy with your honesty. I am ready to give you admission in my college but before that you will have to bring a 'No Objection Certificate' from the Principal of Presidency College."

He received the 'No Objection Certificate' from the Principal of Presidency College.

In 1919 he completed his B.A. in philosophy and took admission for the M.A. course in the same subject. But his thoughts were becoming aggressive day by day. His spiritual thinking and the feeling of social service were getting stronger day by day. His father was watching the changes that had been taking place in him day by day. He wanted to bring changes in his thoughts and for that it was very important to change his environment. He was very keen to build his future in a secure manner.

Three months have lapsed since he began to attend his classes. One day Rai Bahadur Janakidas after consultation with his son, Sharat suddenly put forth a proposal in front of Subhash — "I think you should go to England and appear for the I.C.S. exam."

Subhash was shocked to hear such a sudden proposal. He could not say anything and just stood silent.

"I want to know your decision regarding this."

"But father, I do not want to become an I.C.S."

Subhash, whose mind was in revolt with British, did not want to do slavery for them. Hence he disliked the proposal as it was unacceptable for him.

"What objection you have in becoming an I.C.S?" asked the father to his son. "Don't you want to lead a peaceful & happy life?"

"It's my pleasure? Father, my greatest happiness lies in sacrificing my life for my nation."

"But you still can serve the nation remaining in this service," said the father.

"No father, no. Once my soul gets polluted I will be happy in governing and overruling our own countrymen. Then I won't be able to serve them."

"Then what do you want? What is your ambition in life?"

"We have discussed about it many a times. I know very well that my life has a definite aim. My aim is to revolt against the present. My soul is craving for the rebellion. I do not want to subdue them by becoming a servant to the British government."

Rai Bahadur gave a sarcastic laugh and said, "Keep your knowledge with yourself. Why don't you accept the fact that you don't have the capacity or knowledge to compete with the British?" These were not just words but poisonous arrows that pierced the heart. Subhash could not tolerate these words.

"Father, today Britishers are ruling our country. We are dominated by them, and that is why you are all praise for their intelligence."

Subhash's eyes were shining with self-confidence. "Okay, I will go to London and pass the I.C.S exams."

"Leave it. You better go in the next year. You don't have sufficient time left now to prepare for the exams. Perhaps you won't be able to pass the exam."

These words from Rai Bahadur came as a second arrow piercing his heart.

"Father, Subhash does not know the meaning of failure. I will show my caliber to you as well as to those Britishers, whom you are praising so much. Please make all arrangements for my trip to England at the earliest."

Subhash accepted the proposal to go to England because his self respect had come under attack. But he didn't want to go to England to become an ICS officer. He was desirous of visiting England but not to attain any honorary degree from any of its universities.

This proposal gave rise to a problem for him. Whatever social works he had been planning to do in India would go topsy-turvy. With all these going on his mind he wrote a letter to his friend Hemant Kumar Sarkar:

28/2-Elgin Road
Calcutta
26th August 1919.

I have a very serious problem-before me, yesterday a proposal for sending me to England has been put forth before me. I will have to go to England now. There I am not hopeful of getting admission in any good university. My father and brother want me to study for Civil Services examination for few months and appear for the exam.

My heartfelt desire is to gain a university degree from any of the famous universities in England. If I am unable to do so I will not get any opportunity in the field of learning. If I say that I do not want to go to England to appear for Civil Services examination, then I will lose this opportunity and god knows whether I will get such an opportunity again. In such a situation of indefiniteness, should I let go this opportunity? What is even more difficult is that if I achieve success in Civil Services Examination then I will go astray from my aims and ambitions and I have to give my decision tomorrow itself. Father has returned back to Cuttack yesterday. I have agreed to go to England but I have not been able to take decisions regarding my actual duties and responsibilities in my life. I need your advice if you can come to Calcutta at the earliest.

— Subhash.

Chapter - 9

15th September 1919

Subhash departed to England on ship. Almost all his family members had come to the port to see him off.

The separation was painful but all of them wished a bright future for him.

His friends were worried about his aim. His mother was sad and blessed him with a heavy heart. Her son was going abroad for attaining higher education.

One month and ten days had lapsed since his departure. On 25 October 1919 Subhash reached London.

Now he was worried about his admission. He went to the Indian Counselor's office at Crambel Road, but they could not provide any help for getting him admission in Cambridge.

Some students advised him not to waste his time and go and try for admission on his own effort.

Subhash did not wander much. He met some students from Orissa. One of them introduced him to Mr. Reddaway. He provided Subhash assistance in every possible manner to gain admission in Cambridge. Finally he was enrolled as a student of Cambridge University. He had already missed three months of studies and it was very essential to complete those lessons.

Subhash did not waste even a second. He was very keen to prove his caliber.

Subhash saw many Indian students there and kept a watch on their behavior and activities. He used to feel agitated at their activities. He felt sad after assessing their lifestyle and manners. He thought, India is under the subjugation of British rule and these Indian students are here leading the life of princes. They are hardly worried about their country. Those students are attending parties at big hotels in London and spending time with fashionable and pretty ladies and wasting their money. Subhash was unable to bear such worthless endeavors on the part of Indian students.

One day during a free period Subhash went out of the college. One prince called Subhash from behind. He invited Subhash for dinner with him that night.

Suhash said, "Forgive me Prince. I am not interested to go with people who are not concerned about time or money."

The comment pierced the prince's heart. He felt very bad and said, "What are you talking. I invited you considering you my friend. But you are insulting me!"

"Prince, you feel insulted at what I told you. But do you consider living under another country's subjugation as a matter of pride?"

"I am not anybody's slave. I am the prince of a province. I am not in any way related to any kind of subjugation."

"You are considering yourself the prince of a province but the real owner of your province is the Resident Governor whom your whole family members are paying obeisance. You can rule over poor public, but in buttering the Resident Governor you leave no stone unturned. This lavishness on your part appeases the British because this money is a part of loot from poor Indians. Prince, if you could have understood all this!"

"I will see you later," Prince replied loudly in a challenging tone and went away.

Subhash had come to England to quench the doubts that frequented his mind. He wanted to study the moves of the British in their own country. But his father was feeling assured that his son has gone abroad to become an ICS.

Before Subhash's departure to England, the Jallianawallan tragedy had occurred but they were unable to receive any proper news in that regard. Everyone's mind was brimming up with the idea of revolt.

In 1919 Lokmanya Tilak made a visit to the Cambridge University. There, he, while addressing the Indian students, appealed to them not to take up government job and instead serve the nation.

During those days Subhash had heard that Deshbandhu Chittaranjan Das, an established lawyer, had left his profession and fully devoted himself for the cause of the nation. And in the same country there were several others who were entangled in foreign domination and having received titles like 'Sir,' 'Honorable' and 'Rai Bahadur' were subjecting their own countrymen to cruelty.

During 1919-20 the atmosphere in the country was even more maligned. News of poor condition of people and their agonies were pouring in from all sides. At this junctures Mahatma Gandhi called for the Non-Cooperation Movement. This spread a wave of excitement all over India.

Subhash, though in England, was well informed about the incidents and developments that were happening in India. He felt angered at the thought of his being away from his homeland at that juncture.

The I.C.S. Examination was over. Hence Subhash spent most of his time in thinking about the nation. One day he received a telegram from his friend.

"Congratulations and see at early morning 'Morning Post'."

Subhash was surprised to see in the newspaper that he had not only passed the ICS examination but in the eligibility list his name was in the fourth position.

He was very happy. He has fulfilled the promise he had made to his father. He has left behind the British in this competitive exam. Now the real problem stood before him. He was indecisive of what to do and what not to do. He was unable to decide whether to accept the government job or not. Should he leave his dreams for the sake of this prestigious job and lead a luxurious life or leave this post for the sake of nation's benefit.

Days lapsed in this state of indecisiveness. He was receiving congratulatory letters from all quarters-from his middle brother, father and many friends.

In a long letter addressed to his brother Sh. Sharat Chandra Bose he wrote: 'but I cannot live a life of slavery. I won't do this job.'

In the letter he wrote:

L.N.C. Essex
22-09-1920.

Most reverend brother,

I am happy to receive your congratulatory letter. What good has this passing of ICS exam brought to me? But I am happy that this news has brought happiness for my parents and those close to me.

I am getting congratulatory wishes from all quarters because I have attained the fourth position but I am not feeling happy at all after achieving such a feat. If I have to be a part of this slavery then I will have to do this job unwillingly as I have prepared and studied for this exam.

I am very well aware that this job will assure me a good salary and a good amount of pension as well. If I gain aptitude in the act of servitude I am sure that I can reach up to the level of commission. If I make further efforts in this direction, perhaps I would be able to become the Chief Secretary of a province. But is acquiring a job the sole aim of my life? I will get worldly peace and happiness in job but from where can I get spiritual happiness? In my opinion, every individual belonging to the ICS class while working within the legal limits, if try to stick to the highest ideal is doing nothing but befooling himself.

For a common man this would be an achievement in life and what I am feeling at this moment perhaps you might be able to understand. There are innumerable advantages of this job. One can enumerate so many of them. Every day, there are innumerable people who are toiling hard and worried about making the two ends meet. For such people this is a real solution. There will remain no doubt whether life is a success or a failure, but for a person with my kind of thoughts leading a tension free or fulfilled life is not the ideal way. For those who are not attracted towards worldly comforts and desires, for them doubts and danger are not very frightening. And it is true that once you are entangled with the shackles of Civil Services you cannot really work for the nation. Once you are bound to the rules and regulations of the service you cannot merge your national and spiritual feeling with them.

In all probability you will say that I should not decline to accept this job and should take it up and try to revise it or reform it. There you have a point in saying so, but if we do so, someday the situation will take such an ugly turn or will become intolerable that resigning from the job would be the only way out. If such a situation arises after five-ten years then I won't be able to cope up with it and will try to find an alternative way. At present all ways are open in front of me. Once I accept this job all my capacities and abilities will come to an end.

Again perhaps you will say that I should not denounce this evil path and I must enter it and fight against it. Being associated with the government, enduring their scolding, harming the health, closing other doors of achievements and remaining in this one can do very simple and commonplace things which are insignificant as compared to what I can do by staying away from the job and devoting my complete time to it.

Moreover, the actual question here is about ethics. Ethically I cannot even think of becoming even a cog in this government machinery. This government mechanism is full of heartlessness, cunningness, cruelty and it has deviated from its actual objective.

Now I have reached the middle point of both the ways and I am unable to find any middle path. Now either I will have to completely sacrifice my desires of accepting this prestigious job and devote my whole life for the nation or I will have to denounce my ideals and ambitions and enter the civil services. I know that many people will feel despaired by this obstinacy on my part, but I am least bothered about their thoughts or there praises or admonitions. I have full faith in my ideology and that is why I am clarifying my situation before you. I am confident that in the future I will accept any call for self-sacrifice bravely and patiently.

I have also written a letter to father seeking permission in this regard. I am hopeful that if you agree with my views you will try to convince our father. Your opinion in this regard is really important to me.

— Yours Subhash

Subhash was making up his mind. He had decided that he will not make his soul a prisoner at any cost. But what his aim will be, once he returns back to India was an important issue.

He should decide it at that juncture itself so that he was able to convince his father. And he began his constructive work without wasting any time.

With this objective in mind he wrote lovingly letter to Sh. Deshbandhu Chitaranjan Das:

The Union Society, Cambridge
16ᵗʰ Feb 1921.

Perhaps you do not know me. But after reading about me in this introduction you will be able to identify me. I am writing this letter to you, which is related to a serious issue.

My father Sh. Jankidas Bose is a practicing lawyer in Cuttack and was the government lawyer a few years ago. My elder brother Sh. Sharat Chandra Bose is a barrister in Calcutta High Court. Most probably you might know my father and definitely my elder brother. In October 1919 I had come over to London. In August 1920 I passed the Civil Services Exam with a fourth rank to my credit.

Now I came to the point – I am not interested in a government job. I have already written a letter in this regard to my father and brother. I have not received any reply from them as yet. In order to get their permission I will have to show them what I am really going to do. I know very well that if I kick this job and devote myself completely for the cause of nation, I will have many worthwhile things to do for my country. Such as teaching in the national university; writing and publishing of newspapers, magazines and books; educating the common public etc. But I should make a sure choice and convey the same to my parents and elders so that I get permission for that. If I leave this job with your permission then I can do any work assigned to me by you.

I want to know in this cause of service to the nation, what job you will assign to me. I do not have that much of educational qualifications nor do any intellects but I have the youthful exuberance. I am still unmarried. I have studied Philosophy. I was enrolled for an Honors course in the subject in Calcutta University and in London. I am also doing a research in the same subject from Cambridge. I have attained some overall knowledge due to Civil Services.

I am not able to guess from here what all job opportunities are available in our country. I think that after returning back to my homeland I can devote my time in teaching and writing for newspapers. My desire is to take a clear decision and then leave the job. In such a situation, I won't have to waste time in contemplation instead I can straight away start my work.

You are the main coordinator of the national service in Bengal. Hence I am presenting myself before you with whatever education, knowledge, energy and enthusiasm that I am having in my possession. I have nothing else to lay down for my motherland except for this soul and this insignificant body.

I am waiting for your reply. I am curious to know that what all responsibilities you will entrust me.

I think if I leave the job, I will make my departure from here in the month of June.

Forgive me for my over-expression. I am hopeful that you will make a reply soon.

Yours

Subhash Chandra Bose

Subhash had already informed his father that he had put in his resignation. He received a letter from his father. He had through the letter, made an attempt to convince Subhash. He in his letter wrote to Subhash that he can fulfill his work remaining in Civil Service. He also assured that India will gain independence within ten years.

But all these words had no effect on Subhash. He was not concerned about his own well-being and prosperity and he was not bothered about the new system of governance or its benefit on him. But he was thinking whether or not he will be able to serve the nation remaining in government service. While continuing to remain in this situation, accepting the domination of a foreign government, will it be correct to enter into this deal wherein the soul itself is at state? A kind of duel was going on in his mind and he wrote a letter to his brother.

"Since the day the result of ICS examination has been out, one question is constantly going on in my mind— whether I will be able to serve the nation better while being in service or will it better to leave the job for the sake of the country? Now I have received an answer to this question. Now I have taken a stern decision that I can serve the nation better while in the company of common men. I am not saying that I cannot do any good for the nation by remaining in government job. But in my opinion the kind of service I can do for the nation by keeping myself away from government job will be far better than what I can do while in government service. Moreover I will have to take care of ethics. It is impossible for me to accept the domination of foreign rule. To do public service in a proper manner it is very essential to leave all ways leading towards materialistic development. The example of Arvind Ghosh always remains before my mind's eye. My feeling is that by choosing such a spiritual path I will be able to pay of those debts. And the atmosphere and the environment around me are suitable to fulfill my heart's desires."

Self respect and self-sacrifice both the motions were instilled in his mind.

He was so confident- "The day I sign my appointment letter, I will no more remain an independent person."

In Subhash's opinion-"If we pay the full price, then we will be able to achieve complete independence before ten years. And that price is self-sacrifice. Self sacrifice and self-penance is the only way of attaining freedom. If we get entangled in the nuances of a job and we fix our attention on personal gains then we won't be able to attain freedom even in fifty years.

Subhash felt that if not every individual; at least one member from a family should completely devote his life for the sake of motherland. Someone or the other should make this sacrifice. If somebody else had voluntarily come forward to take up the job I would have backed out but the situation is not so and the valuable time is lapsing out. The time has become ripe to present an example in front of others.

Now Subhash had taken the final decision. He will not accept the ICS at any cost. He made up his mind— "After signing the appointment oath whether I work for three years or three days, that does not make any difference. But the mere act of signing the document will result in my downfall and destruction of my principles." And on 22 April 1921 Subhash finally put in his papers, surrendering the prestigious ICS.

There was a turmoil and turbulence in the Indian office situated in London. Such an incident had taken place for the first time in history.

Subhash faced personal pressures from various quarters. Sir William Duke, Ex-Commissioner, Cuttack tried to influence Subhash and rethink about his decision but in vain. Mr. Swart, Secretary, Civil Service Board Cambridge, also asked Subhash to reconsider his decision. But Subhash was firm on his decision.

Chapter - 10

On 16th July 1921 after almost two years Subhash returned back to his homeland.

The 23 year old youth who had mentally, physically, spiritually decided to denounce his life for the sake of his country. He had become a point of discussion among every one.

Subhash had chalked out some plan and wanted to meet some national leaders, discuss the same and know their views regarding it.

He had already made up his mind to meet Mahatma Gandhi and the very same day he met Mahatma.

Mani Bhawan—Gandhiji was sitting on the carpeted floor

with his face towards the door. The room reflected a Khadi look. Gandhiji welcomed young Subhash with a sweet smile on his face.

Subhash's mind was full of questions. He expected a satisfactory reply for all his questions. He wanted to know what all mechanisms Gandhiji wants to employ to get rid of British rule. What are his plans?

Subhash opened a box of questions in front of Mahatma.

During the conversation he received a satisfactory answer to only question.

Gandhiji understood his actual problem and asked him to meet Desbandhu Chittaranjan Das after getting back to Calcutta. Subhash was very keen to meet him from the beginning. He had received a reply to his letter from Chittaranjan Das when he was in London.

When he went to meet C.R.Das, Subhash was surprised to see the changes that had come over him. Those days came to Subhash's mind when he was studying in college and he was expelled from the college and he had gone to meet C.R.Das. The image of young Barister Chittaranjan Das who earned thousands of rupees in an hour came before his eyes. Now he was even more sympathetic towards youth. His behavior was very friendly. Subhash accepted Deshbandhu as his leader.

Deshbandhu also experienced a strange caliber, skill in Subhash. Deshbandhu was greatly attracted towards young Subhash's sense of patriotism and self-sacrifice. He appointed Subhash as the teacher of a school founded by him.

In 1921 the meeting of Indian National Congress Committee was organized in Bailwada wherein it was decided to launch the Non-Cooperation Movement with added vigor. It was also decided that one crore volunteers be selected and trained and Rs. one crore be collected towards 'Tilak Swaraj Fund.' After returning back to Calcutta from the Indian National Congress Committee, Deshbandhu began the work of enrolling volunteers at a large scale.

Subhash was appointed the Chief of these volunteers and the volunteers began to be imparted training on daily basis. The British government was scared. The youth organization was working with a strange kind of enthusiasm.

People were discontented and displeased by the foreign government. Discontentment spread all over the country and revolts and rebellions were uprising in various parts of the country against the British rule.

At that time the government announced the visit of Prince of Wales to India. Subhash was the leader of the Congress Swayam Sewak Dal. Subhash firmly opposed the visit of Prince to India.

The government was taken aback by the success of the strike called by Congress Swayam Sewak Dal. The fear was evident from the news and articles being published in the newspapers. Government announced a ban on Congress Swayam Sewak Dal calling it an illegal organization.

On 1st December 1921 the Bengalis gave an enthusiastic beginning to the Non Cooperation Movement. The whole atmosphere gave a feeling of strike and rebellion. Many Congress leaders were arrested. Government was trying to subdue the revolt and end the revolt immediately.

Subhash was also arrested along with Deshbandhu Chittaranjan Das. The court ordered a punishment of six months in jail. Hearing the punishment meted out to him a smile came on Subhash's face and he asked the magistrate— "Only 6 month's imprisonment?"

This was Subhash's first jail visit. While going to jail he told his mother:

"Pray to God that mothers of India give birth to sons like me and every house gets purified with the presence of a mother like you. Every drop of my blood sows the seed of independence in every house."

Chapter - 11

In the year 1922, Deshbandhu Chittaranjan Das chalked out a very significant plan. He was of the opinion that if one of their chosen representatives is elected and send to the Council, then the reigns of governance can be easily kept under the control of Indians.

In the same year during the 37th session of the Indian National Congress, Deshbandhu was the Chairman of the meeting and he presented his plan before the other members. But the supporters of Gandhiji opposed this proposal and the plan was shelved.

Subhash as well as Pt. Motilal Nehru was also present in the meeting. The opposition increased and difference of opinion rose heads within the Congress Party.

Motilal Nehru floated a new party called 'Swarajya Party.' Deshbandhu C.R.Das formally resigned from the Congress Party. Now he was free to critically analyze the policies of the Congress.

Swarajya Party organized mass movements rapidly. Under the leadership of Subhash day by day the mass movement gained momentum. Entry to the council became the topic of discussion everywhere. The Swarajya Party began to publish a daily newspaper named 'Forward.' Subhash was entrusted with the administrative supervision of the publishing of the newspaper.

Subhash wrote comments and articles which inspired the public and instilled enthusiasm in the minds of people.

In March 1924 elections were to be held in Calcutta. Swarajya Party decided to contest the Municipal Council elections.

Congress strongly opposed this. But will power and public cooperation were also strong forces working in favor of Swarajya Party. In spite of opposition from the Congress Party, Deshbandhu C.R.Das filed his candidature in the election.

Swarajya Party emerged victorious. Out of 75 seats, Swarajya Party gained victory on 55 seats. Deshbandhu Das was elected the Mayor of the city. Subhash was appointed the Supervisory Officer of Calcutta city. At that time Subhash was just 27 years old.

Revolutionary changes were brought about n the working of the Municipal Council. Subhash was getting instructions from his great leader and he was engaged in practically applying those instructions.

For the first time the citizens of Calcutta city feel that the employees of the Municipality were actually meant for their service. It was made mandatory for all employees to wear *khadi* clothes.

Subhash himself applied 50 percent cost cutting in his salary. Instead of the actual salary of Rs. 3000 he accepted Rs. 1500 as his monthly salary. He diverted his complete attention and devoted his time to make improvisation and public service.

British government was scared by the popularity of Swarajya Party and people's attraction towards Subhash. Government considered these revolutionary developmental works as a revolution in Indian mind. The foreign government could not bear the spreading of any such patriotic move and began making plans to counter them.

Chapter - 12

In October 1924, Lord Lytton passed the 'Bengal Ordinance Act'. Under the act many political leaders were imprisoned. Even Subhash was arrested without any valid reason.

Subhash remained in Berhumpur jail for some days. From there be coordinated the activities of Calcutta Municipality. A CEO was appointed in place of Subhash, but he collected information with the help of his brother Sharat Chandra Bose and gave instructions and suggestions regarding various activities being undertaken by the municipality form the jail itself.

After a few days Subhash was sent to Mandley jail. Mandley jail was the real empire of dust, pollution and disease. There the atmosphere remained dusty throughout the year because it never rained in this part of the world.

In one of the letters addressed to Shri Sharat Chandra Bose he wrote- "There is dust everywhere in Mandley jail. There is dust even in the air. Hence while reciprocating we are compelled to breathe the dust in. There is dust in the meal, so we intake dust also while eating. Here dust storm is a constant feature and the dust envelops the trees and mountains all over. The atmosphere here gives a feeling of stagnation. The ailment of joints becoming rigid is quite common here."

In such an environment like cattle shed this lion man was kept. His ward was made of wooden planks. One can easily imagine what he must have experienced when he was locked in that wooden room.

But memories of Lokmanya Bal Gangadhar Tilak were associated with the Mandley Jail. He spent many years in this jail. These historical memories of the jail gave Subhash peace and he remained pacified. He felt— "This is a place of pilgrimage for me because a great Indian had spent six years continuously in this jail."

Subhash lost his weight considerably due to the fever. He wrote an application requesting the authorities to shift him elsewhere from there but his request was not considered. The officers thought that Subhash was saying a lie. Subhash suffered all atrocities in silence.

It was at this juncture that Subhash received the news of the death of his favorite leader Deshbandhu Chittaranjan Das. It was an indeed a shocking news for him. Subhash went into a semi conscious state for a second. The person on whose directions he has been undertaking this important task is no more with him. The person, who used to rain the warmth of love and sympathy on these youngsters, has left them. This was the heights of sorrow. At that moment Subhash forgot his physical illnesses.

Smt. Basanti Devi, wife of Deshbandhu Das had always showered motherly love on Subhash whenever he met her. He wrote a letter to her from the jail, which describes the helplessness and pain he suffered at the loss of his beloved leader:

Mandley Jail
6th July 1925.

Mother,

Regards! Today at this hour of misfortune, I, the imprisoned Bengali, am sending this condolence message. The kind of sorrow being confronted by you at this moment is the greatest of all the sorrows confronted by a woman. But it is my misfortune that when you need my support, I am not near you or your family. In this hour of distress, if my words even reach you, I will consider myself great and will feel satisfied. The one who has left this earthly abode was very much near to my soul. Today the whole of Indians are feeling bereaved at his departure. But the Bangali society as a whole and youth society in particular is the one who is actually feeling the brunt of this irreparable loss.

His kith and kin, his friends of his childhood, teenage, adulthood all are weeping for him. Those unlucky, untouchable people for whom he distributed his wealth, those for whom he devoted his mind, life, health and age, all of them are in a state of mourning. But how is it possible to express the feelings of those youngsters of Bengal who had assembled under his flag; those young men who obeyed his orders in happiness sorrow, light and darkness; those who got themselves involved in the freedom struggle and sometimes enjoyed triumphs and sometimes experienced tribulations behind the jails; those who never left his company in hope or despair; those who found a father figure, a comrade and a teacher in him! Life of Deshbandhu, like the sun in its Prime, set in the middle age.

Deshbandhu left this earthly abode. That blessed son of the almighty God left the vast work field called India wearing the crown of victory. Today he attained eternity due to his patriotism. Now we are experiencing darkness around us, in the outside world and our heart is filled with a sense of vacuum. The darkness has enveloped us in such a manner that is not even a bit of space left for the entry of rays of light.

I remember those days when the sky of Bengal was pervaded with the dark clouds of despair. The brave hero of Bengal was put behind the prison. A strange and powerful image took charge of Bengal and on that day Bengalis not only considered you the heroine of Bengal but raised you to the pedestal of the mother of the state.

Hence my humble request, to you mother, is to pacify us in this hour of distress. The darkness in which the nation is completely covered at this hour, the sorrow that golden land of Bengal is experiencing who will give it a new lease of life, new power, and new excitement other than you? The way you instilled life in the veins of Bengalis, in the same way spread awareness among them. The whole society of Bengal will supplicate before you. With your blessings they will attain success in the battle field.

Bande Maataram!

Yours
Subhash

Chapter - 13

Durga Puja is a significant festival of Bengalis. Every Bengali celebrates this festival with great fervor.

Subhash was in jail but he decided to worship Goddess Durga with complete devotion. He sought some allowance for the purpose from the jail authorities, but in order to crush the National Movement, the authorities bluntly refused to entertain the request.

Subhash was greatly infuriated at this incident. He sat on hunger strike till death. His declaration of hunger strike shook the whole nation. This gave rise to a huge public revolt and mass movement all over the country.

A proposal for suspension of proceedings as put forth in the Central Assembly. Speaking in connection with the proposal Sh. T.C Goswami said, "The reason for this hunger strike is not that the prisoners are not being provided with the necessary arrangements for Durga Puja, but they are facing difficulties in many other ways. Life of Subhash Bose is in danger. If he dies in the hospital the government and Home Secretary will breathe a sigh of relief but the loss the whole of India will experience, who is going to fulfill that?"

The proposal was passed and renowned leaders sent a request through telegraph to Subhash to end his hunger strike. The whole nation offered prayers and wishes for his good health.

The request that Subhash received from all over compelled him to end his hunger strike after six long weeks on 4 March 1926. Subhash's health was deteriorating day by day. Those were the symptoms of Tuberculosis. He looked very week. He was shifted to Rangoon jail. The officer in the Rangoon jail Major Flower Dew also ill-treated and insulted Subhash. He strictly ordered that Subhash cannot make communications with the outside world through letters or any other means. The tone and language of the jailer was indeed insulting for a person like Subhash. But Subhash behaved in a very padtient manner. He just said— "I have been in jail for many days and I am aware of all this."

Here also nobody bothered about his illness. He showed his temperature chart to Major Flower Dew and said "I am having fever." At this the Major replied: "Where is the temperature?"

Subhash was kept aloof from other prisoners. The other prisoners were threatened of dire consequences if they kept any kind of contact with Subhash.

Day by day the jailer's behavior towards Subhash became all the more crude. He complained about the cruelty being meted out to him to the governor of Burma in two lengthy letters which he wrote him:

"As per the laws of the country I am under house arrest and I am entitled for a better behavior in accordance with my post and status. Hence I feel that the Superintendent of Rangoon jail Major Flower Dew has hurt my sentiments and has insulted me in front of his lower subordinates. His statement is objectionable, unmannered and insulting in every aspect for an intellectual person. At this moment I am not able to decide how I should behave with the jail authorities. What I feel now is that it is better not to write anything to the jail authorities and sacrifice all my needs and requirement otherwise I will have to face even more insults."

On 19 March this fight became even more severe. Subhash was worried about the negligence and irresponsible attitude of the jail authorities towards him and his health. He informed about this to Pt. Motilal Nehru, Sh. J. N. Sen and his brother Sharat Chandra Bose and asked them to make request to government to transfer him from this jail.

Subhash was transferred to Insin Jail.

His body was thoroughly crumbled due to weakness. Now he felt difficulties in sitting and getting up as well. The government medical officer and his brother Sharat Chandra Bose checked him thoroughly and stated that his health was a cause of deep concern.

On the other hand Moberley, on behalf of Bengal government, put forth the proposal to let Subhash free and send him to Switzerland for recovery from illness. For this, two pre-conditions were laid down. First, before the completion of Criminal Law Amendment, Subhash cannot return back to India, secondly, the ship in which Subhash will leave for Switzerland; it will not stop at any port in India.

This condition was indeed insulting. Subhash was furious. The government was going to the promise of Subhash's recovery but with so many conditions attached to it.

Subhash could easily recognize government's actual intention behind such a proposal. The government wanted Subhash to leave for Europe and once he left India they would make Criminal Law Amendment Act a permanent feature so that Subhash can never return back to his motherland.

Subhash declined the offer and expressed his views to his brother Sharat Chandra through a letter:

Insin Central Jail
4th April 1927

Reverend Brother,

You will be of course curious to know my mind regarding Mr. Moberley's proposal to send me to Switzerland. I feel that the time is ripe to express my views in this regard. I read Mr. Moberley's proposal more than once. I have contemplated on every word and every sentence said by him. I should rather appreciate Mr. Moberley for creating such a view with such care and caution. Though I decline the proposal due to the following reasons, I accept some honorable parts of the proposal.

First of all I want to clear all the illusions associated with it. Whatever brother, Dr Sharat Chandra Bose has mentioned in the report being published, I have no role in that. He never sought any suggestions or advices from me as to what he should write in the report. If I had known what he was going to write in the report, I would have vehemently opposed the proposal of sending me to Switzerland.

When he told me about it after sending the proposal, I had my doubts that its outcome would not be good. It is true that brother Sharat came to check me but I am sure that he behaved like a true doctor and scientist. But I feel that government instead of accepting the remedial measures put forth by him accepted the need of change of weather. It is quite evident from Mr. Moberley's remarks—'Subhash is not seriously ill, nor he is very weak, nor is he incapable of doing any work.' I am very curious to know when the government will accept the fact that I am seriously ill and that I am incapable of doing any work. Will they accept it when some doctor will declare that it is impossible for me to recover from this illness and that I will die within a few days? Moreover if they are not ready to accept the treatment being recommended by brother Sharat, then why are they so keen to support his recommendation of sending me abroad for recovery? I don't think that dada Sharat must have supported them in their endeavor of not letting me meet my near and dear ones or not meeting them before leaving for Switzerland.

He also did not say that even if I recover from my illness, as long as the ordinance is valid, I will not be permitted to return back to my country. Seeing all this I have my doubts that the government is not actually very keen about the recovery of my health.

Moberley had said the truth that only two ways are left— either I remain imprisoned in jail or I go abroad for change of weather and remain there for an indefinite period.

Then really there is no middle way between these two extremities. But I don't think so. Government desires to keep me in prison till the expiry of the Ordinance that is January 1930. But who can say that this ordinance won't be enforced again after January 1930. I won't be surprised if the government starts its efforts to revive this ordinance in 1929 itself. If such a thing happens I will have to remain in a foreign land forever. If the government had any clear cut objectives in this regard, they should have written in their proposal and mentioned the date when I will be able to return back.

They have also not made anything clear about the level of freedom that I will get during my stay abroad. Switzerland is full of detectives and how will the government save me from their clutches. You cannot deny the fact that I am a convict of political conspiracy and as long as I do not change my views and project myself as their informer or detective, the government will always have doubts regarding my integrity. In all probability the government will depute a detective behind me and my life will become intolerable for myself.

I know that police detectives show more interest in such topics. Even if I stay in Europe in a peaceful and careful manner, they will send illegal reports to the Indian government. Even if I do not do anything mischievous, they will consider me a conspirator and give derogatory reports against me. There are possibilities that before 1921 they will declare me a great Bolshevik leader and with that all means of my returning back to India will be closed. It seems that Europeans are afraid of Bolsheviks. Due to all these reason I am not willing to move out from my own country.

Mr. Moberley's statement shows his heartlessness. Government is well aware that I have been imprisoned for almost two and a half years and during these years I have not met any of my relatives, not even my parents. According to the proposal put forth by the government I will have to stay abroad for at least two and a half or three years. During that period also I won't get an opportunity to meet my parents. Of course, this is very painful for me. But for those who love me it is even more painful. Westerners cannot even imagine how close knit relationships people of East share with their friends and relatives. In my opinion it is out of ignorance that they have displayed such a heartless behavior. In their opinion I am not married and I do not have any family, hence I am not very much attached to anyone else.

Perhaps the government has forgotten what all I suffered during these two and a half years. I suffered a lot but they did not. They kept me in prison for long without any reason. I have been told that I am accused of supplying arms, ammunitions and other explosives and murdering a government servant.

After my arrest the government has not made any arrangements for looking after the people who are dependent upon me nor safeguarding my household. When I wrote letter in this regard to the higher officials they just suppressed it. And now I am being asked to stay abroad for another three years. And during my stay there I myself have to make arrangements for my living expenses. I am not able to understand such a proposal full of contradictions. The government should at least be responsible for freeing me at least in the same health condition when I was imprisoned in 1924.

If the government allows me to go to my home before leaving for Europe, bear the expenses of my trip, and let me return back to India without any objections once I recover, then it will be a gesture of goodwill on the part of the government.

If such a thing does not happen, I have made up my mind that instead of being expelled from my motherland forever it will be far more better and honorable to remain in the jail and accept death.

Whatever I wanted to say in defense and in opposition I have said. Nobody needs to worry about the delay in my gaining freedom. I know that mother and father will be very sad. Hence, pacify them. Before gaining freedom we will have to undergo much of personal and social sufferings. I am thankful to the Almighty God that I am staying here peacefully and I am getting myself prepared for the acid test. My redemption lies in sacrificing my life for the sins committed by the whole nation.

Our views and ideals will never die. Our value will be embedded in the memories of the society. In future our posterity will become the heir apparent of these principles. With this belief I will be able to endure all sufferings and sorrows with a smile on my face.

Yours affectionate
Subhash

How could that brave heart accept banishment from his country? Instead of going abroad he would have sacrificed his life. He thought—

'To me life is not so dear that for it I chose cunning ways. My thought regarding death is entirely different from what people normally have. My view is that physical well-being or personal success is not the yards to measure success or failure of a human being. The objective of our revolt is not to attain physical strength or power. The ideal aim of our life is to attain freedom and achieve truth. In the same way as day dawns after night, our efforts are true and truth always triumphs. Our body may perish but victory will be ours because we have with us the assets of self-confidence and determined sprit. God only knows who will be the lucky one to witness the results of our efforts. Regarding me I can only say this much that I will keep on fulfilling my duties, whatsoever their outcome be.'

Government was well aware that the health condition of Subhash was deteriorating. Hence, they considered it right to free him before the outbreak of any public revolt, so that he may regain back his health according to his desire and will.

Chapter - 14

16th May 1927

The whole nation was overjoyed. Subhash Bose got freedom. But at that time he was just a structure comprising of bones.

Meetings were organized at various parts of the country in honor of Subhash. The mood of festivity prevailed all over. For the whole nation he delivered a message:

"Now I have returned back to my own country. My first duty will be to regain back my health so that I can continue with the noble task entrusted upon me."

Subhash was a person with great strength and will power. Within a short span of time he regained back his health and became robust as before. Nobody had imagined that he will be as healthy as before and all his well-wishers were very happy.

During the three years of imprisonment Subhash was away from active politics. Once he regained back his health, he was elected the President of Bengal Provincial Congress Committee and once again he devoted himself to active politics.

3rd May 1928

The sixth session of Maharashtra Congress was held and Subhash was made the Chairman of the session. People were awe inspired by the speech of their young leader. Subhash expressed his acknowledgement for making him the Chairperson of the meeting. He said that earlier he was not ready to accept the invitation but the sweet relation between Bengal and Maharastra prompted him to accept the invitation.

In the meeting, Subhash said, "The foreigners are of the view that the awakening of India was the result of its ideologies. But it is not true. At this moment I do not want to kick start any controversy regarding it. Whether the influence of western thoughts have awakened our spirits or not, but its influence have helped us in awakening our self-esteem as this Freedom Movement is the result of that. For a long time India had been in the grip of blind faith and superstitious beliefs. But now it has upgraded its spirit and is working towards rebuilding of its national ideals."

Subhash clarified— Democracy is not the product of the West. It is a human institution. Wherever human beings have tried to develop political institutions, suddenly this institute of democracy has arisen. The ancient Indian history is full of examples of democratic institutions.

Democratic set up of government is prevalent in many parts of India. For example, the *Adivasis* (tribal people) of Assam elect their leader at the consent of all the members of the community. And this tradition is being followed since ancient times. In certain towns and villages also democratic ideology is being followed.

Some people consider nationalisms as of narrow ideology as compared to cultural globalization. They consider nationalism to be selfish and violent. But in my opinion nationalism is neither narrow nor selfish or violent. It is inspired from the famous ideology of '*Satyam, Shivam & Sundaram*'.

Indian nationalism has given us the emotions of truth, honest, humaneness and sacrifice. More importantly these emotions have awakened our creative talents which were in deep slumber for such a long time. All this have resulted in a renewed energy in various art forms of our country.

Friends, I want to tell you that you should keep your eye on the future along with the present realities and see how clear it is!

As far as I am concerned I am a supporter of an independent sovereign state. And that is my sole aim. India will build its fortune and will not be happy with foreign domination. Why should we be under the domination of British Empire? We have manpower and other physical resources in excess. India has crossed its childhood stage imposed by foreign domination. Now it can fulfill its own responsibilities as well as work in an independent manner.

It is baseless and unnatural to say that India cannot defend itself without the help of Britain. Even today, the Indian army as compared to the British army can very safeguard India's interest. When Indian army can fight battles on foreign lands such as Tibet, China, Paris, Egypt etc. for the sake of Britain, then undoubtedly India is fully capable of fighting against any kind of foreign invasion.

After remaining under British domination for such a long period, it will be very difficult for Indians to overcome its feeling of hatred towards the British. As long as we remain a part of British governance, it is difficult for us to oppose them.

If we want indeed to make India a great nation, then we should establish a democratic political state based on our democratic ideals. The advantages one gets by birth, caste and creed should be abandoned and everyone should be given equal opportunity to develop his skills and talents.

Different religious communities should be aware of each other's tradition, ideals and history because cultural affinity and unity can only bring out communal harmony and integrity. Political unity can be achieved only through cultural unity.

Religious fanaticism is the greatest hindrance in the way of cultural unity. The only way to root out this evil is impartial and scientific education. This kind of education will lead to economic independence. Economic awakening will result in the destruction of religious fanaticism.

Friends, my request is to support youth-awakening and youth-movements. Youngsters will not only perform their duties but also will be imaginative and creative. They will not only cause destruction but will also be instrumental for new construction.

Dear friends, we have reached the most sensitive part of our history and it will be to our benefit, if we accumulate all our strength and take a strong step against these foreign powers. We should join our hands and heart together to achieve freedom and independence.

Chapter - 15

December 1928

It was the 45th session of Indian National Congress in the city of Calcutta. Pandit Motilal Nehru was presiding over the session. Everyone was worried about the future of India. Many leaders warned the British government. Pt. Motilal Nehru had accepted the proposal of provincial government.

Mahatma Gandhi had put forth the proposal that if the British government does not hand over power to provincial government, Congress will start Non-violent Movement.

But Subhash didn't like this. He desired to attain complete independence or 'Purna Swaraj'. He was never interested in attaining the dominion status.

Subhash put forth an amended proposal and said:

"I am sorry to make amendment of the proposal put forth by Mahatma Gandhi which has the support of many experienced leaders.

I feel that we should not be ready to delay the unfurling of our flag of freedom for even a day. As far as the young generation is concerned, they are ready to take up the responsibility of independent India. We love our leaders and have affection and respect for them but we want them to move ahead according to changing situation. If our leaders do not strike proper coordination with the views of the young generation then there are likely to arise big differences. The youth of the country have achieved novel ideas and they cannot imitate others blindly. They have realized that they are the heir apparent of the future India. They are the ones who are responsible to achieve freedom for India. With this new awakening in their minds, they are all ready and prepared to face any difficult situations.

One more argument in favor of this, which I feel is very significant, is the international situation. You all must be remembering that after the Madras Proposal India had achieved a special position in international politics. Now I am afraid that with the acceptance of this proposal we will lose the honor we received after the Madras Proposal.

In the main proposal you have given twelve months time to the British government. Are you sure that you will be able to attain the powers of Provincial governance within such a short span. Even Pt Motilal Nehru has expressed his doubts in this regard. Then why should we restrain ourselves from unfurling our flag for twelve months. Why should we not say that we are fed up of British administration and we have no more faith left on them and we are keen to take some extreme step against them?

In all probability you will be keen to know what good this proposal of 'Purna Swaraj' will bring out. My belief is that it will help in the development of a new mentality. After all what is the cause of the deterioration of our politics! It is our mentality. If you want to win over this slavish tendency, then you should encourage your countrymen for complete independence. Even if we are not able to fulfill this hope of ours completely, by getting across this expectation of 'Purna Swaraj' we may lay down the foundation for creation of a youthful and energetic generation.

But what I want to say is that we are not going to sit idle. I have already told you that the young generation is very well aware of their responsibilities and they are well prepared to face any kind of challenge. We should consider the complete programme and should employ our entire capability in fulfilling our plans so that our proposal is not thrown into the dustbin.

Before concluding I would like to draw your attention to one fact. All the incidents are pointing towards the possibility of outbreak of World War because all ingredients necessary for outbreak of war is present in the world today. Countries are competing with each other for accumulation of dangerous weapons. In fact all independent nations are preparing themselves for a new war. In such a scenario we should mentally prepare our countrymen for 'Purna Swaraj.' It will be possible when we declare our views and ideals in a clear-cut manner.

The moment national movements rose in our country, we had defined freedom as complete independence. We never meant it to be a dominion status. The idea of dominion status is least acceptable for us. This is not acceptable for even the younger generation who are in the stage of development. We should remember that the youths are the future heirs of our nation.

It is my final submission and request that if we accept this amendment, then our leaders will not have to face any disgrace. Respect, love and reverence to our leaders is a different matter but respect of our principles is much different from that. You are requested to accept my proposal and give a renewed momentum to the new generation."

With this amended proposal put forth by Subhash Chandra Bose Congress split up into two groups. One group opposed the amendment and other group supported it. A tug of war arose between the two groups. Pt Jawaharlal Nehru supported the amendment. Though the amendment proposal received a set back with only 973 supporters as compared to 1350 opposing members, it became evident that the stance of the left was powerful.

But Subhash was very adamant in his resolve. He was least affected by the incident. The proposal failed not due to the opposition of the members, the reason of its failure was the indefiniteness in their minds. They were thinking that if Mahatma Gandhi confronted opposition he will leave politics and the members of the Congress Party did not want Gandhiji to leave the party.

The Calcutta session was ended. The amendment proposal became invalid but Subhash did not sit in silence.

Every citizen of India became an ardent fan of Subhash. The love and respect he received from the public increased his responsibilities towards the nation. The image of a slavery, poverty and timidity of the nation persistently haunted Subhash. He wanted to redraw a beautiful and attractive image of the nation.

He formed and founded many youth organizations with a view to instill patriotism and thus awaken them from the slumber of shackles. Sardar Bhagat Singh was the leader of youth organizations based in Punjab and northern India. He founded the All India Youth Organization and gave a new lease of life to armed revolutionary movement.

25th December 1928

The third session of the All India Youth Congress was organized in Calcutta. In the welcome address he accorded a warm welcome to all the representatives of the youths from various provinces.

With his exuberant speech he addressed the youth and said- "If we peep out from our limitations and look at the happenings around the world, we will come to know about an interesting thing and that is the reawakening of the young generation. All around us we can experience the reality of youth movements.

Wherever the leader from the old generation have experienced failure, the young ones have become alert and have played an important role in the reconstruction of the society and have proved their mettle in accomplishing the task in a successful manner.

Dear friends, let us talk about things that are happening near us. Not only the youths of Germany, Russia, China and Italy have awakened from their slumbers, but the reamers of this dreamland have also awakened. I am sure that this awakening has originated from its roots and it is not a superficial one. The youths of India are no more ready to put all the responsibilities on the shoulders of old leaders or they sit idle or follow their leaders like cattle following their owners. They are clear about their objectives of building a powerful and new India. They have accepted their responsibilities and are ready to face any consequences. They are totally engrossed in fulfilling this significant responsibility and indulge in training themselves. I am not the one among those who is ready to forget our glorious past. We should make the past our base. We have a culture of our own which we should develop according to our needs and within our moral and ethical values. We have so many new things with us in the form philosophy, literature, art and science which we have to give to the world and the outside world is waiting for them. If I say it in one word, we have to unify the modern with the ancient. Some of our good thinkers and leaders have already started with this significant work.

It is very difficult to exercise ethical control over momentous movements. But I am sure that if the leaders who are showing us the way or leading us remain in the correct path, then the outcome will also be right."

To give a new momentum and awakening to the whole nation Subhas coined a new slogan "*Complete Boycott.*"

On the Lahore session of Congress in December 1929 he said, "My programme is overall boycott. I don't think that there would be any good in boycotting a single aspect leaving all others. Either you should practice complete boycott or do nothing. I am an extremist and my principle is either everything or nothing. If I support the capture of any government institution, then I would expect to capture all of them. If we have to practice boycott, why not boycott everything?"

The British government was thoroughly shaken by the support that Subhash accumulated from youths, laborers, farmers etc. The coward and unjust British government found the dangers inherent in the gaining popularity of Subhash and he was falsely accused of treason and arrested along with some of his supporters on 23 January 1930.

He was sent to jail for a year. In the meantime government put forth a proposal before Subhash. He read it and tore it off.

The proposal was not to participate in the Freedom Movement for a year. If he accepted this proposal he would have been released from prison. But such a proposal could not lure Subhash in any manner. He declined the proposal and was happy to go to jail.

He said, "The government only imprison our body but the fire deep inside is ready for inflammation at any point of time."

Chapter - 16

1st April 1931

An All India Political Prisoners meet was held at Karachi under the chairmanship of Subhash Chandra Bose.

Subhash said in the meeting— "No civilized or educated person would ever like to stay in jail because the conditions prevalent in these jails are enough to turn a person insane and inhuman. During a person's imprisonment no one can gain any mental or ethical development. Infact he experiences a complete moral and ethical degradation. The system in Indian jails is a blind aping of bad ideals.

Beating the prisoners for petty offences, behaving with them like animals, blowing small incidents out of proportion and insulting them would not be of any help in putting a curb on their criminal tendencies. Today such cruel activities are going on Indian jails. Political prisoners are also treated like social offender. All efforts are being made to put their morale down. They are leaving no stone unturned in corrupting their character. In such circumstances, a person freed from prison after his punishment would prove to be an evil for the society. He would be experiencing a complete downfall— morally and mentally.

In such a dangerous situation wherein the prisoners do not have appropriate facilities of accommodation or food, how miserable his mental and physical situation would be, is beyond imagination."

Subhash further said, "My dear friends, after seeing the condition of jails, I feel pity for the inmates of those prisons. Instead of extending them with a psychological treatment, they are being subjected to inhumane physical punishment. The untimely death of late Sh. Lokmanya Tilak is a clear indication to the miserable condition of Mandley jail.

We should kick start a mass movement to compel the government to improve the conditions of jail. We should begin with the proper course of treatment so that conditions do not further deteriorate beyond control.

Chapter - 17

During those days the Gandhi-Irwin pact was signed. Many political prisoners were released as per the conditions of the pact. The pact seemed to be in favor of Indians but it was not so. But the bureaucratic mentality was quite evident everywhere. Officers were left free to torture anyone. Ill-treating people became one of their additional duties.

Subhash was furious to see the miseries of the people. He was aggrieved by the atrocities being made on poor people. His mind was preparing for the revolt. He disliked the moderate thoughts of Congress. He developed a feeling of distrust toward the activities launched by Congress leaders. Till now he had his doubts regarding the capability of these leaders in influencing others. But now it is evident that the Congress leaders have just learnt to mould themselves according to the circumstances, they were not able to mould others. Just four days after Sardar Bhagat Singh was hung to death, the All India Youth Congress session was held in Karachi. In its presidential speech Subhash said—

"The basic weakness inherent in the principles and programmes of Congress is that the minds of these leaders work only thinking of their own benefits. Their minds are unsystematic and their thoughts are unclear. Their programmes are not based on improvisation but on mutual agreement. Their agreements are the ones that happen between a landlord and a tenant, a capitalist and a laborer, a higher class and a lower class, a man and woman.

I don't believe that these activities and endeavors on the part of Congress will help India attain independence. In my opinion we can attain freedom only by adopting the following methodologies.

(1) Get the farmers and laborers united.

(2) Organization of voluntary teams under strict discipline.

(3) End of casteism and uproot of all sorts of social and religious superstitions.

(4) Organization of women institutions under a properly chalked out principle and planning.

(5) A mass movement to boycott all sorts of foreign articles.

(6) Design attractive literatures to disseminate or propagate all these newly chalked out programmes."

After this he said, "In my opinion, the Gandhi-Irwin pact is the most disappointing agreement between Indians and British. I am extremely saddened by the fact that we have entered into such a pact at this juncture when we are in a powerful situation. In fact this pact is full of weak points, but since we have signed the pact we should look into the possibilities of exercising our duties. Now the only thing we can do is to do something creative so that our nation becomes all the more powerful. To achieve this objective, I have put forth outlines of some programmes which I have in my mind. These programmes will help the Congress leaders in regaining their losing popularity and will stop the further weakening of our nation and strengthening of our enemy. Instead of insulting others we should exercise patience. If we practice patience and kindness, we will gain something good than bad."

Subhash once again emphasized, "The focal point of all the current happenings around the world is India and independent India can wipe out the imperialistic tendencies all around the world. Hence we should set ourselves on the path towards freedom that we can save humanity."

People were already fed up by the cruel behavior of Lord Wellington. After this speech by Subhash, the fire of revolt spread throughout the nation like wildfire. Subhash's words reached every nook and corner of the nation. Subhash's slogan: 'Do something constructive and creative' entered into the Indian minds. A general sense of hatred pervaded the minds of Indians.

The mass movement that began at the call of Subhash was increasingly threatening the British administration. The Viceroy of India and the Governor of Bengal were overcome with fear by the increasing popularity of Subhash.

A government memorandum was published and on 2nd January 1932 people of India came to know that Subhash has been arrested. Government could not put any specific blame upon him. The memorandum only stated that Subhash is a revolutionary and he has spread the web of rebellion all over the country to topple British government.

From then onwards Subhash began to be considered as a political prisoner. During those days the atrocities against the political prisoners were subjected to be of beyond description.

Once again inside the prison, Subhash's health deteriorated. The government was so overwhelmed with the fear of Subhash that they were reluctant to even free him for his treatment. After much effort he was send to Bhuvalic Sanitorium but his health did not improve. He suffered from stomach pain, time and again. This brave leader almost lost 400 pounds of weight in this duration.

In this condition the medical board at Bhavali and civil surgeon of Lucknow recommended him to go to Switzerland or France for change of weather and early recovery.

Still the government did not take any decision for a long time. When Subhash's condition worsened and the government felt that he will not be able to survive, then the government woke up from its slumber. They suddenly realized that if something happens to Subhash it will result in the outbreak of a nationwide revolt. Then the government gave Subhash the permission to go abroad for treatment.

Subhash wanted to remain in his own country like a free bird. Hence he was not a bit happy at the prospects of going abroad. But he was compelled to go abroad for the sake of his health.

Subhash was prohibited from meeting his parents even while going abroad. This shows how much the government felt threatened by Subhash. They considered him a dangerous revolutionary. They were afraid that if they let Subhash go and meet their parents in Cuttack, he will escape from their clutches.

In a government notification it was said- "Subhash's meeting with his parents as declared as a nonsensical act. They interpreted it as a plan on the part of Subhash to hoodwink the police and escape from the police to continue his anti government activities in hiding." The official who circulated the above notification wrote— "I am sure that Subhash's mother and father are not going to die in the near future. And the fact is that if Subhash had not been going abroad and would have remained in jail, then also he would not have been granted permission to meet his parents. Then why is he so keen and desirous of meeting his parents now? Moreover it is impossible to send Subhash to Cuttack under police protection as it will prove to be dangerous for the government."

How an inhumane a decision was this!

How much afraid the government with Subhash!

Chapter - 18

13th February 1931

The ship on which Subhash was going abroad left the Bombay port. Those who assembled there to see him off were not even let to meet him. His heart wept and tears came to his eyes.

The worshipper of freedom, Subhash was distanced from his motherland. He stayed in Venice for sometimes, and then he was sent to Switzerland.

After reaching abroad he also restarted his work. He kept on expanding his contacts. During those days a conference of students from East was organized at Rome. Subhash inaugurated this programme. On the occasion Mussolini addressed the students at the Julius Ceaser Hall.

After staying in Rome for few days Subhash went to Poland. At Warsaw he saw that Polish people were very much impressed by the Indian culture and civilization. Subhash gave a scholarly speech at the Oriental Society.

After this he came to Geneva. From there he went to Nice (a place in southern France). The weather and environment there really helped Subhash to regain his lost health.

29th September 1933

The third International Conference relating to India was held at Geneva.

Representatives from America, China, Denmark, England, France, Germany, Holland, India and Switzerland participated in the Conference.

Subhash gave a meaningful speech in the Conference. He said, "If somebody wants to know the current condition of India, then first he should surely know the kind of suppressions going on there. No need to explain the condition of those who are in jail. Even worse, those who have been freed from jail are also facing restrictions and prohibitions of one kind or the other from the part of government. Their presence outside has made no difference in their situation.

At this moment the Indians are sitting calm, but their silence does not mean that they are afraid of this suppressive policy and they have accepted defeat. The feeling of attaining freedom is deeply embedded in the minds of Indians and as the unlucky Indians are denied this basic human right, it is impossible to extinguish the fire of revolt in their minds.

The question of independence of India is not the problem of India only; it is a problem of the entire world. The British rule in India is the basis of British empire and which in turn is the foundation of world imperialism. Hence we should constantly make efforts for India's independence and thereby for the independence of the whole world."

Chapter - 19

Janakidas could not even meet his son. Subhash was sent abroad with so many restrictions. He had suffered so many atrocities at such a young age and as a result his health had deteriorated. The father thought that his son will gain some health benefits; hence he restrained himself from reacting in any manner.

But he was anxious about his son, as a result of which he became ill. His health deteriorated day by day and he had become very weak. It seemed that his death was quite evident. In such a situation a telegram was sent to Subhash informing him about his father's serious condition.

Hearing the news of his father's illness, Subhash was very much worried. His fury towards the cruelty of the government get flared further more. But he himself was in a helpless situation.

His own health condition was not very good. But ignoring his own illness, he decided to reach India to meet his father on death bed without any further delay.

Indians got the information of Subhash's homecoming.

4th December 1934

When the aeroplane descended the Dum Dum Airport, lakhs of people were present there to receive him. As soon as the people saw the glimpse of their beloved leader, loud cheers echoed the airport.

But as soon as Subhash alighted from the aeroplane two sergeants took him over and did not let him meet anyone.

He was taken to his home in a closed car. The atmosphere at home was very strange. A queer kind of silence enveloped all over.

Subhash was unable to bear such a miserable situation. He went inside and touched his mother's feet. Then he moved toward his father and seeing his condition, tears came rolling down his eyes.

This was that very Subhash who never lost his balance in any situation. But now seeing his father on death bed he lost his control.

Babu Janakidas opened his eyes slowly; which was very keen and longing to see Subhash. It seemed as if he was waiting just to meet his son before leaving this earthly abode. Seeing his dear son, his lips shivered a little but he could not say anything. Subhash felt as if the whisper being made by his father had some godly message inherent in it. And he began to weep like a child. Everything was over by then.

He came out of the room with tears in his eyes. He was surprised to see that his house had been surrounded by police on all four sides.

He was given an order wherein he was instructed to remain within the four walls of his house and not to go outside. And the communications that he made through post should first be shown to the police officer before sending it; otherwise he will be imprisoned for a period of five years and also penalized.

He was subjected to such an inhumane behavior. On the one hand he was already distressed by the death of his father and on the other hand the restrictions imposed upon him restrained him from sharing his feelings with anyone.

But the government was not satisfied with this much. Just after the lapse of two days he received another order in which he was instructed to go back abroad or else he will be again arrested.

Subhash was in a dilemma. He wanted to stay behind till the completion of all religious rituals associated with his father's death. He asked for one more month leave.

Subhash felt that he had not completely recovered from his illness. The symptom of his illness was evident on his face. He had become very weak and he could not even properly attend the people who took part in his father's funeral rites.

In such a situation it became compulsory for him to go abroad. It seemed that without surgery his recovery was impossible.

Chapter - 20

All arrangements for his surgery were made at Vienna. On 10th January 1935 Subhash departed for Vienna in a ship named Victoria.

Earlier also Subhash had propagated the condition of India and the suppressive policies of British government over Indians. This time also he could not sit idle while in the foreign land. He was not so bothered about his health. For him the mission was important, hence no sooner than he felt better, he engaged himself in some activity or the other.

He presented the true picture of India before the foreigners and tried to enhance the image of Indians before others. The British government had drawn a false picture of India to the outside world. Subhash proved everything wrong and made them aware of the true political and economic scenario in India. During his stay abroad he visited Berlin, the capital city of Germany. In his message the Mayor of Berlin said, "We heartily welcome the Mayor of Calcutta Mr. Subhash to Berlin."

Subhash reached Ireland via Paris on 3rd January. At Ireland a welcome function was organized in honor of Subhash. The newspapers published the news of Subhash's arrival giving it much significance. Irish Broadcasting Corporation invited him for giving a speech on India.

The head of Irish democracy D.Belera met Subhash at Raj Bhawan and expressed his sympathy towards the freedom struggle by Indians. This meeting between D.Belera and Subhash was a cause of grave concern for the British government.

To keep a control on each and every letter sent by Subhash a detective was deployed but all this had no effect on Subhash.

During this journey Subhash wanted to go to London but the cowardly British government did not give him permission to visit England. Perhaps they were afraid that Subhash's magical words will influence the people of London.

Subhash was now feeling that his health had improved. He wished to comeback India. He was longing to meet his countrymen. He was not able to collect information regarding what is happening in India. His longing to visit India increased day by day.

He sought permission to return back to India from the government but the British government declined his request. The government told him that if he wanted to stay in India then he will have to remain in jail.

Now only two ways were open before Subhash. Either he would spend the rest of his life in this manner in a foreign land or stay in his own motherland in a jail and sacrifice his life for the country. He decided what course of action he should take and informed his decision of returning back to India to all his friends.

The government also came to know about this and was shocked to hear the news.

8th April 1936

Innumerable people crowded in Bombay to welcome Subhash. All of them were keen to have a glimpse of their beloved leader who had been exiled for years. People also knew that the government will arrest him as soon as he alighted from the ship.

Loud shouts of slogans echoed the whole atmosphere. As soon as he came out from the ship the government handed over to him his arrest order. This time also he was not allowed to meet anyone. He was once again put behind the bars without any reason. This act on the part of the government spread the fire of discontentment among the people.

The worries and tension of the government increased instead of getting decreased.

Subhash was kept in dirty and unkempt prison. The cell in which he was kept had no proper ventilation from where he could get fresh air.

It was the severe hot summer season in the month of April. The walls of jail heated up like a brick kiln but the jail authorities were least concerned about the health of this national leader. They were only worried about the fact that if this revolutionary leader was set free he will once again spread and encourage revolutionary mass movements. Hence, they kept Subhash imprisoned for their own welfare.

In the unhealthy environment inside the jail, once again his old disease cropped up. Within a few days his health condition deteriorated and become a cause of worry for all alike. He suffered from fever, indigestion and acidity which made him uncomfortable.

This heartless and cruel gesture on the part of the government made the whole nation furious. On 10th May 1936 the Congress President Pt. Jawaharlal Nehru called upon the nation to observe Subhash day.

In an awe-inspiring speech at Prayag, Pandit Jawaharlal Nehru said— "The arrest of Subhash is not only the issue of denying out beloved leader's freedom but the question of principle is also attached to it. And every patriotic Indian, whether he belongs to a political party or not, should join hands together to fight against this trouble and injustice caused by government's one sided decisions and also to safeguard individual's personal liberty."

The mentality of the government was quite surprising. Neither it filed a case against Subhash in the court of law nor had any plan to free Subhash.

The whole world was keen to free Subhash from the atrocities be suffered inside the jail. Demands of freeing Subhash from jail poured in from all quarters and from all over the world.

In such a situation the government was compelled to rethink over the matter. They felt that if they exercised further delay in freeing Subhash they will have to face insult and shame from all over the world.

In order to save themselves from such a disgrace, on 10th March 1937, the government freed Subhash unconditionally.

Chapter - 21

In February 1938, the 51st session of Indian National Congress was held at Haripur (Gujarat). On the banks of Tapti River the Vitthal town was established. The whole town was lightened up with electric bulbs. During this session the political career of Subhash was rechristened. Subhash was made the chairman of the session.

Subhash was taken to the venue of the Congress session in a huge procession. He was made to sit on a chariot being drawn by 51 bulls. As he reached the venue, Gandhiji also reached there in a car. When Gandhiji alighted from the car, Subhash lent him a helping hand and helped him to walk up to the stage. The enthusiastic crowd welcomed their beloved leaders with huge sounds of applause.

Subhash Bose gave an enthusiastic and scholarly speech. In this historical speech he called his fellow countrymen for the reconstruction of the country:

"The main problem that we are likely to face in the process of reconstruction of our country is that of poverty. It would be essential to make fundamental changes in the present land system so as to put a curb on poverty. Undoubtedly, removal of *Zamindari* system will also be very essential. The loans taken by farmers should be waived off and the village folks should be given loans at a much lower rate of interest. Scientific methodology of agriculture should be adopted so as to improve crop production."

Emphasizing on the importance of farmer's associations he said—

"In order to maintain discipline within our organization, we have to give a serious thought to another problem which had been a cause of indifference earlier also. What I mean is the relation between trade unions and the Congress. Two contradictory opinions exist in this regard— one in which all other organizations with the exception of Congress are considered dangerous and the other in which independent organizations are given complete support. In my opinion we cannot break those institutions by insulting or ignoring them. Their existence is extremely evident. Their governance has been established and there is no sign of their getting destroyed. It is very much clear that some historical power is behind them. Such organizations are also present in other countries. Whether we like them or not we should accept their existence. Now the question is—how the Congress is going to treat them? What we should keep in mind is that whether these organizations are against the Freedom Movement of the Congress party or not. Hence the Congress party should try to impress and influence them to follow our ideals and ways. Congress workers should ensure maximum participation in the meetings of farmer unions and labor unions. With whatever experience I have with labor unions, I felt that we can be a part of such unions without getting involved in any kind of arguments or oppositions. The cooperation between Congress and these two unions will no more be complex, if they specially relate themselves to the economic demands of the laborers and farmers and consider congress to be the most powerful organization whose objective is to cut the shackles of foreign domination."

Subhash further said, "Today, we are fighting against difficult situation. There is difference of opinion within the Congress among the leftists and rightists, which should not be overlooked. Today, British imperialism has put forth a challenge before us. In such a dangerous situation there is no need for anyone to remind us about our duties and responsibilities. We should face this storm strongly and be instrumental in defeating the unjust laws of our cruel administrators. Congress is the most appropriate weapon to win the battle of freedom. There may be extremists in it as well as followers of non-violence, but both should get united under the shadow of Congress and fight against imperialism.

In the end, as I conclude, I wish that Mahatma Gandhi stay alive for a long period and our country progress under his able leadership. And this is the wish of the whole country. India does not want to lose Mahatma especially at this moment when unity among people is of prime importance. We want his presence to avoid any kind of hatred ill- feeling during this battle for freedom. We need him for the sake of humanity. Our fight is not just against British imperialism but against world imperialism. Hence we are not only fighting for India, but for the human race as a whole. Attainment of independence by India means freedom of humanity from all kinds of fears."

After the Haripur session Subhash coordinated the Freedom Movement with great dexterity and complete devotion.

Chapter - 22

After the Haripur session a renewed spirit and enthusiasm was evident in the Freedom Movement. Some significant achievements he made during his tenure as Congress President was the formation of National Planning Committee under the presidentship of Jawaharlal Nehru, which he coordinated himself.

The forthcoming session of the Congress was decided to be held at Tripuri. Arrangements began for the election of new President. The extremists supported the nomination of Subhash for another term.

Gandhiji recommended the name of Dr. Pattabhi Sitaramaiyya. A strange kind of conflict had arisen and both the sides competed vehemently against each other. Many big forces worked against Subhash. This time Pt. Jawaharlal Nehru also worked in opposition to Subhash. The whole country was closely and curiously watching the election clash between their leaders. All were doubtful whether Subhash will win or not in such a circumstance.

On 29th January 1939 when the result of the election was out and Subhash emerged victorious, even an idealist like Mahatma expressed his fury and annoyance at the outcome. Expressing his displeasure at the outcome he said, "Defeat of Dr Pattabhi Sitaramaiyya is my defeat."

On 10th March 1939, early in the morning, a procession of the newly elected President was held. Subhash was unwell so he did not participate in the procession. In his place, his photograph was placed which was drawn by 51 elephants. The procession started from Madhia near Pisanharia (around 9 KM from Vishnudutt Nagar).

The tricolor was hoisted on the chariot and photographs of all the 51 past presidents of the Indian National Congress were kept on 51 elephants. The procession ended at Jhanda Chowk.

Subhash was very much unwell. In his presidential speech he said— "My request to my countrymen is to end mutual fights; accumulate all our resources and utilize it for the freedom movement and make use of the present opportunity which is suitable to accomplish the mission of attaining independence."

Subhash also talked about the Rajkot Agreement as well as ending of Gandhiji's fast. Talking about his election as the President and referring to the resignation of first row leaders of the Congress he said— "The election of the President was not simple, many aggressive events occurred during the election process and 15 members of the working committee tendered their resignation. An important member of the working committee, Pt. Jawaharlal Nehru though did not tender his resignation but circulated such a statement which made every individual believe that he has tendered his resignation."

Discussing about domestic politics Subhash said, "Whatever I have been experiencing for the past few days, I feel it pertinent to make clear. Now the time is ripe to put forth the demand for complete self-rule *(Swaraj)*. It is now time to present our national needs religiously before the British government.

What I feel is that the problem is not when union government will be imposed upon us but the problem is what we should do when we are offered with the option of union government. We should put our national demands before the government like threaten and should give them a specific time period for fulfilling the same. As soon as the time period gets lapsed we should put up a challenge before them.

There are many people in Congress who are pessimistic and think that time is not yet ripe to attack British imperialism. But in the real sense I do not find any reason for this pessimism. The congress is in power in eight provinces because of which our national freedom movement has achieved a great deal of success.

We should bring awareness among the people of native states. This is very essential. There is no better opportunity than this to get on the path of attaining Swaraj, especially at this moment when the international situation is quite supportive."

Emphasizing on the importance of unity Subhash said, "If we forget all our differences and utilize all our resources completely engaging ourselves in the freedom movement, then we can attack on British imperialism without any resistance from their side. We should earn as much profit as possible from the current circumstances and show our political foresightedness."

During the session Subhash had difference of opinion with many veteran Congress leaders. Subhash wanted to attain Swaraj from the British government within six months. He suggested starting the Freedom Movement if the British government does not fulfill the demand put forth by them. But Mahatma Gandhi was of the opinion that the time was not appropriate for the Movement.

The difference of opinion between these two great leaders kept on increasing. The job of the Working Committee also became very complex. No creative or worthwhile task got accomplished. Subhash requested Mahatma Gandhi to revamp the Working Committee but Mahatma Gandhi did not pay heed to it.

Subhash was witnessing the rift that was taking place within the Congress. He did not want to be a reason for the crumbling of such a big party. After much contemplation, on 29 April 1939 in the meeting of the Congress Working Committee, he tendered his resignation.

On 16th may 1939 a grand meeting was organized at Hazara Park in Calcutta. In this meeting he gave a glimpse of his mind about his resignation from the post of Congress presidentship. Analyzing the complete circumstances from beginning till the end he said—

"The election to the post of President was against what I had thought, in every sense. But it made the mind of general public and Congress members crystal clear regarding their allegiance. With my victory, Mahatma Gandhi gave a statement, which influenced many Congress men who trusted Gandhiji more than the Congress Working Committee and withdrew their support to me. Undoubtedly, a huge number of Congressmen, who do not like the Congress Working Committee, were not ready to leave Mahatma Gandhi.

When I met Gandhiji in Wardha on 5th February, he suggested me to form the Working Committee without the old members. I discussed with him about this at great length and requested for the formation of a mixed committee. At the end of this discussion, I assured him that I will somehow convince Sardar Patel and other members to remain as members of the Working Committee. Mahatmaji told me that if I can do this, he does not have any reservations against it.

But unfortunately my illness served as an obstruction in the accomplishment of this plan and I was unable to meet the members of the Congress Working Committee in the meeting held at Wardha on 22nd February. On that day all the senior leaders submitted their resignation. After this, what all happened in Tripuri you all are well aware.

After the Tripuri congress I became so ill that I could not even meet Mahatma Gandhi. He asked me to go and stay in Delhi but my doctors made it impossible for me. They informed about my condition to Gandhiji through a telegram and advised me to do my work by means of postal communication. After a lapse of almost a fortnight when I felt that my health is a bit improved, and then I felt that through letters, work is not being done in the proper manner. Then I thought of meeting him personally. I was so excited about my meeting with him that I decided to travel all the way to Delhi ignoring even my doctor's advice. Unfortunately Mahatma Gandhi had to go to Rajkot and thus we could not meet each other.

After that I met Mahatmaji at Calcutta on 27th April. His thoughts were still the same as was evident in his letters or as expressed by him at the Wardha session. He was still insistent upon forming a new Congress Working Committee leaving those members who had resigned. For some reasons I did not follow his advice because a Working Committee formed by new members will never be able to attract the trust of Mahatma Gandhi and it would have been against the condition laid down by Pandit Panth. This committee would have been against my thoughts because I believed that, for the interest of the country, we should form a committee comprising of both old and new members. Hence time and again through letters and messages I requested Mahatmaji to declare the names of the Working Committee members during the Tripuri session considering his responsibility.

When in Calcutta Gandhiji completely refused to take up this responsibility obstacles began to be created. Now there was no other alternate than to put up the issue before All India Congress Committee. In such circumstances I was asked to discuss the matter with Dr. Rajendra Prasad and other members of the Working Committee and make efforts for making representatives for the formation of new Working Committee. I told Gandhiji that I can accomplish this task with pleasure. If my efforts had been successful, I would have presented that agreement before All India Congress Committee for formal approval. But unfortunately we were not able to reach any agreement in this regard. Now the question is why we failed in our efforts and who is responsible for this failure?

I began my discussion first and foremost with Dr. Rajendra Prasad. I put forth the proposal of including four members and recommended the names of those four. After discussing about it for some time we went to Maulana Abul Kalam's house for further discussion in this regard. There I was told that the names recommended by me were not acceptable. Instead new names were proposed and Pt. Jawaharlal Nehru's name was proposed for the post of Chief Secretary. I accepted this proposal and requested Pt Nehru to accept the post. Before we could take any final decision in this regard, we had to postpone our discussion for a conversation with Mahatma Gandhi.

When we resumed our discussion, again an entirely new proposal was put forth in which it was stated that the old Working Committee members be appointed once again. In my first discussion what I could make out was that there was no difference of opinion regarding the appointment of four new members and nobody would oppose any particular name. But I became doubtful when I see that the new proposal was supported by Mahatma Gandhi. I was told that two posts will be vacated after some times and two of the names suggested by me will be appointed then. When I accumulated further information in this regard, I came to know that I can appoint only these two members. When I wanted to know why these two members could not be appointed in the beginning itself, the reply to my question was in negative. In order to further clarify the matter I asked whether the members whose names I have proposed will be appointed in the vacant positions and I proposed my names also, but both the names suggested by me were unacceptable.

Then I asked whether I could nominate one of the members suggested by me as the Second Secretary who will be based in

Calcutta. I made it clear that in the beginning there is a need for 3 secretaries, from which I have recommended two names—one for Allahabad and one for Calcutta. And indeed it was necessary for getting assistance for my work. But this time also my proposal was rejected.

When we reached such a situation in the course of our discussion, I told Mahatmaji that it is very much clear that none of my proposals will be accepted. When I am not getting any support for my views from the other end, how will I be able to work? I did not want to remain like a show piece nor did I want to stay in the post without any work. So I tendered my resignation from Congress Committee so that a new President gets elected in my place and a new Working Committee is formed at the earliest. I do not have any doubts regarding my decision.

Many a times I have repeatedly said that I have submitted my resignation with a supportive spirit and it will prove to be beneficial and advantageous for the nation. In order to avoid the danger looming over the Congress Party and when all efforts of mutual agreement failed, to uphold my self-esteem, honor and my duties towards my country I felt it better to tender my resignation."

The turn that all these incidents have brought all the Indians unhappy. In this regard the editor of the famous daily newspaper 'Aaj' wrote a comment:

'Our respected and senior leaders should have worked with an open mind. Gandhiji has earned a high pedestal in the hearts and minds of every countrymen and his honor would have remained untarnished, if his followers behaved in an open minded manner. But nothing of the sort happened. I feel sorry that whatever happened was not only detrimental but also has proved to be harmful for the senior leaders as well as Gandhiji.'

In the end, the Working Committee had to accept Subhash's resignation and after that new members were elected for the Working Committee.

Chapter - 23

May 1939

Subhash Babu established the 'Forward Block'. When he established this party, he had two expectations from it—Be well prepared and smart to deal with the problems that may arise with the rightist members of Congress and to gain the confidence of Congress with its views.

He also decided that if he is not able to gain the trust of Congress and the Congress fails in its mission then Forward Block will continue with the struggle at its own end.

Conflict between the rightists and Forward Block continued.

In June a committee of Left Front was formed in which members of Socialist Labor Group, Kisan Sabha and Forward Block assembled. Subhash was entrusted with the task of coordination of this committee. In the meeting of All India Forward Block, members of all the parties assembled. In the meeting, it was emphasized to begin the freedom movement at a larger scale all over the country."

June 1939

The meeting of Congress High Command took place in Bombay. The High Command ordered every Congressman throughout the country that without the permission of Provincial Congress Committee they should neither start nor participate in any of the movements.

Subhash propagated a detailed view on this and called upon the people of the country to begin a movement against this proposal. They fixed 9th July for organizing this boycott.

Pt Jawaharlal Nehru termed it as audacity. In his statement he said, "We have built up the Congress with immense love, hardship and justice. This kind of boycott is an open challenge for us. If we uphold this means then our institution will get destroyed. The movement against imperialistic forces will receive a set back and mass movement will convert into conflicts of the party and group."

On the day of 9th July 1939, veteran Congress leaders and workers were in a mood of excitement. They were waiting to see the opposition cum demonstration Subhash was going to put up against Congress and how far he will be successful in his attempt. They were thinking that the entire public is with them.

All this confidence proved baseless on 9th July. On the day boycott and demonstration against the policies of the Congress was organized throughout the country. The demonstration made it clear that people can no more stick to non-violent policies and that soon they will be turning revolutionary. They want to begin a revolt and want a revolutionary leader.

With this successful attempt on the part of Subhash a new excitement spread all over.

The leaders of Congress were taken aback by this victory of Subhash. The popularity and success of Subhash were hard for them to digest and a cause of concern for them. The Congress High Command brought out a declaration stating that disciplinary action will be taken against those members of the Congress Party who participated in the demonstration called by Subhash.

On 11th July 1939 the All India Congress Working Committee meeting was held at Wardha. In the meeting disciplinary action was taken against Subhash.

In a strange kind of proposal passed against Subhash, who was the President of the Congress for twice, he was declared ineligible to be elected to any of the posts in Congress Working Committee for three years.

Commenting on this punishment of expulsion Subhash said, "I warned the country for not going ahead on the path of improvement, but they opposed the Congress' destructive policies against revolution and tried to organize the Leftist Front and at the same time they appealed the countrymen for exercising caution in face of the looming dangers. And just for doing this I have been meted out such a harsh punishment. I am not worried about it at this moment. I will work for the Congress with all the more vigor and vitality. I will still work for the nation considering myself to be a humble servant of the Congress and the country."

In September 1939 the world witnessed the Second World War which had its efforts on India also. In Subhash's opinion it was the perfect time to start a movement against the British government. Congress was not ready to start a sudden movement against the British but Forward Block wanted to begin the movement outright.

Subhash knew that the British government was scared by the terror spread by Hitler and at this juncture a revolutionary mass movement seeking India's independence would not be easily tackled by the government.

On 30th September 1939 Subhash went to Prayag. He shared his opinion with Pt. Jawaharlal Nehru. There he addressed a large public and while explaining about the international scenario expressed his thought regarding the matter.

"We should make the utmost profit from the present situation of the British government. By choosing the correct path we will soon be able to attain Purna Swaraj (Complete Independence). Some people say that we should feel satisfied and pleased by whatever little we gain from British government. But in my opinion we should apply our minds and chalk out a proper plan so that we should achieve complete independence not a partial one. We should not beg for governance but with our unified strength, revolution and patriotism we can win our freedom. That day is not very far when the intimidated government will supplicate before our feet and begs for peace and in return will entrust us with freedom."

Subhash undertook a journey all over India. In fact he was laying the foundation of revolution in the minds of Indians. The nightmarish Hitler and the revolt lit by Subhash disturbed the sleep of the British government. The provocative speech by Subhash was having a surprising impact on the Indian citizens. It was but natural for the government to feel worried.

No sooner than the battle began in Europe, the Viceroy of India, without consulting the Indian leaders or considering India's interest declared India's participation in the War. Subhash Bose and his Forward Block opposed this one sided decision by the government. He started an anti-war campaign throughout the nation.

When the British government saw that Subhash and the members of Forward Block were hindering its war-intentions, Subhash and some of his followers were arrested under the law of safety and security of India.

Chapter - 24

November 1940

Subhash began a hunger strike against his unlawful detention. He told government officials: "Free me or I will give up my life." With this he circulated an appeal for the countrymen –

"No sacrifice will ever go meaningless. For the successful accomplishment and development of any work, patience to suffer difficulties and a sense of sacrifice is very essential. This law is applicable for every era and every part of the universe. The blood of the martyr is the seed of religions.

In this materialistic world everything gets destroyed but thoughts, ideals and dreams never die. One person dies for one philosophy but that philosophy after his death passes on to several generations. The chariot of progress moves in this manner and the dream of one generation passes on to the next like a legacy. Without facing hardship or sacrificing life no thought gets materialized.

I want to tell my countrymen that there is no curse like slavery. Always remember that compromising with injustice and torment is the greatest of all sins. Remember your duty is to fight against injustice even if you have to pay a price for it."

Subhash became very weak due to the hunger strike. On December 1940, because of his ill-health he was freed from the jail by the British government.

Though he was freed from jail but on the pretext of proving security to him he was kept under house arrest.

Government ordered to put an end to many of the comforts provided to him.

❑

PART – II

One

After 1935 it was becoming quite evident that the world wide battle and the incidents related to it had a great impact on the world. The leaders were thinking that if England get entangled in the World War, India will also be compelled to take part in it. In such a situation all the Indian political leaders will be put behind the bars and during the War period-they will be kept in prison lest they oppose the government.

Exactly the same thing happened. The British government began to arrest political leaders one by one and send them to jail. Subhash was still under house arrest.

Keeping in view the future of the country, Subhash had only two options before him. One was to accept the fate and continue being under house arrest during the long war period or escape from India and shake hands with the enemy countries of British and with their help build up an army to fight for freedom.

But it was not very easy to choose any one of the options. There was a dual thoughts taking place in the mind of Subhash. He minutely studied the developments taking place all over the world and contemplated on the impact of all these happenings on India.

Police had laid almost a trap around Subhash's house. There were around 62 police personnel deployed in the area adjacent to his house to keep a watch on him.

He was not even permitted to come out to the verandah. He was not allowed to meet anyone, not even to his relatives. He was not allowed to make any postal correspondence and the letters that were addressed to him were first read by the government officials before being handed over to him. Many of his letters were not given to him stating political reasons.

Even he had no access to newspapers, so he was totally unaware of the happenings inside the country and in the outside world. He was totally fed up of this helpless situation.

Suddenly change became evident in his behavior. He refrained from meeting even his family members. Gradually, after some days he ceased to come out from his bed room even. His niece was the only person who entered his room and that too to give him food. The room was divided into two portions for worshipping and one portion for sleeping and eating.

Subhash chalked out a very surprising plan to free the nation from foreign domination. Now he spent most of the time in meditation and no one got even a slightest hint about his plan.

Two

27th January 1941

Suddenly the news spread like wildfire that in the night of 26th January, Subhash fled by befooling the guards deployed to keep an eye on him.

This sudden disappearance caused a stir throughout the nation. The government could do nothing but be remorseful for such a serious lapse.

The lion had freed itself from the cage. Now the administration had to accept this truth. Famous detectives and spies were employed to search him out. Every town and city was put under search but no one could find Subhash.

The train bound to Peshawar. A Muslim priest (*Maulavi*) was already seated in the compartment. He was wearing a tight pyjama, pump shoes, long kurta (*sherwani*) and a turkey cap. His beard was very long and at the first sight looked like a *Moulavi* from Uttar Pradesh.

A Sikh army man also boarded the same compartment. The army personnel asked the *Maulavi* about his whereabouts.

In the first instance he tried to evade the questions put up by the Sikh personnel and acted as if he was very much engrossed in his reading.

Second time when the army personnel again asked he replied, "I am a resident of Lucknow. My name is Jiyauddin. I am the organizer of an insurance company and is on a trip to Rawal Pindi."

The matter ended somehow. But the *Maulavi* could not sit relaxed. Whenever the train approached a big station he covered his face with the newspaper on the pretext of reading it and nobody was able to see his face. Nothing special happened on the way. The train reached Peshawar at the stipulated time. The car was waiting at the station and *Maulavi* sat on the car after alighting from the train and reached his destination.

Three

The plan continued to be accomplished. After two days Subhash in the guise of a Pathan left Peshawar along with Rahmat Khan and another friend.

They reached a small village called Garhi and spent the night there. At the dawn of day break, Subhash along with Rahmat Khan and two Pathans carrying gun left for Kabul.

Now Subhash had turned into a person with speech and hearing impairment.

By the evening all of them crossed the border of India and reached a small independent village where Pathans live. There at a famous place called 'Adda Sharif' one old Muslim priest (*Peer Baba*) had made all arrangements for them.

All of them were very tired as they had travelled through hilly and mountainous regions. All of them spend the night at the mosque of the *Peer Baba.*

The next day they got up early in the morning. They had not gained sufficient rest but it was necessary for them to leave the place. They had their morning rituals hurriedly and got ready for the next journey.

They reached Lalpura at seven in the evening. Lalpura is a small village. There also every arrangement was made before hand. As they were very tired due to continuous journey, all of them soon fell asleep.

There the arrangement for their stay was done by a renowned person called Khan. He earned a reverential position with the Afghan government.

The next day, as Subhash and his friends were leaving the place; he handed over a letter to them and said that with this letter they will face no problem, wherever they travelled within Afghanistan.

In that letter it was written that "Jiyauddin and Rahmat Khan Azad are the members of the clan and I know them very well."

The way was very tough and it was very necessary to reach there. Hence, overlooking all hardships they faced en route, they continued with their journey.

They were unable to decide whether they should choose the common road leading to Kabul or the short route. Both the ways were prone with difficulties and dangers. Those going through the common road had to show their passports at three places and while going through the short route they would have to cross a river without any bridge or boat.

But look at their indomitable spirits, their desire for freedom: they crossed the river and reached a place called Jhangi. From there they plan to take the help of trucks to reach Kabul.

Rahmat Khan waved at trucks from morning till evening but none of them were ready to give them lift.

Luckily by the evening one truck driver readily agreed to take them to Kabul. The truck was fully loaded with boxes. The driver asked them to sit on the boxes quickly.

The truck began to move at great speed. They really had to sit alert to save them from being hit by the branches of road side trees. The cold climate and the chilling winds made them really shiver. They didn't have any warm clothes with them but somehow they spent the night in the truck itself suffering the chill.

Next day, by the evening, Subhash and his friend reached Kabul.

Four

Two unknown patriots were standing in an unknown country. In such a chilling climate they were not able to decide as to where to go. There was no acquaintance from which they could have sought any help.

Then Rahmat Khan asked a passerby about any inn where they could stay. He showed them a nearby inn.

Both of them reached the inn. The condition there was not suitable for human existence. There were camels, donkeys and horses all over. For sometimes they felt as if they were befooled.

But at that moment they were in dire need of such a place where they could rest for a while.

They enquired one person who happened to come there at that moment about the in-charge of that inn but he could not give them any satisfactory reply.

Somehow both of them search out the guard of that inn and with the blessings of god they got a room. More than a room it was like a prison cell even worse. If they closed the door, one hand could not find the other hand.

By the evening, Rahmat khan arranged some clothes, wood and candles. The winter season in Kabul is very chilling especially in the months of January-February when there is heavy snowfall there.

A market place in Kabul.

There was snow everywhere. Very few people frequented the Market. A Pathan entered the radio shop. He was wearing a khakhi shirt and pathani waist coat. He was looking like a member of the Azad clan.

The shopkeeper asked him what service he needs.

In return the person shot another question back at the shopkeeper— "Is your name Uttamchand?" Such a sudden question surprised the shopkeeper but he gave the reply— "Yes, my name is Uttamchand."

Pathan glanced over the shop and seeing a boy standing there he became silent. The thing that he wanted to say stopped at the lips.

The shopkeeper measured his predicament. He was curious to know what this Pathan wanted to say but stopped due to the presence of his servant boy. Till now everyone used to say important things in front of his servant. Still he sent boy to bring tea.

This gesture made the Pathan pleasant. He said— "I am an Indian. I have come to Kabul with some political motive. At present I am facing a problem. And I need your help to solve it."

"Who are you? How did you come to know about my name? What is your political motive? What problem is being faced by you?" Uttamchand shot back so many questions at a go.

Pathan replied— "My name is Bhagat Ram. I am a resident of District Mardan, village Galladher. I know you since the time you were the General Secretary of Navjawan Bharat Sabha. Everyone in Galladher village knows that your uncle runs a shop in Kabul and you work there. I am here with some objective in mind and you will be surprised and shocked to hear it."

Uttamchand's curiosity kept on increasing. He was interested to know Bhagatram's mission. So he interrupted him in the middle and asked— "Tell me what help you want from me. I can readily provide you with any kind of help."

"I have brought Netaji Subhash Bose along with me to send him to Russia."

"Subhash Bose!" Uttamchand exclaimed, he could not speak anymore. He fumbled for words, and then continued, "Subhash Babu, here in Kabul with you?"

"Yes, Subhash Bose is right here in Kabul and we both are staying in an inn. There a CID Inspector has come following us and is creating problem for us. Subhash Bose has sent me to you for help and has requested you to make some arrangements. It is around 12 days since we have reached here. The very next day a police personal has started keeping a close watch on us and has already extorted a good amount of money from us. Due to our helpless situation we have been fulfilling all his undue demands. I have been hoodwinking him all these days saying that Subhash is my elder brother who is both deaf and dumb and that we are on our way to visit Sakhi Sahab. But we cannot continue with this excuse further. Hence some arrangement should be made at the earliest. In such a difficult situation please do help Subhash Babu."

Uttamchand, after hearing all this, was in a state of utter shock. He was utterly speechless. He had heard some days before that Subhash had escaped from his house by hoodwinking the security personal. After that he had heard in radio that he had been arrested in the guise of a saint from Haridwar. He also read a statement by Shardool Singh in the newspaper that "In my opinion he has gone to Southern India in the guise of a saint," But now when he heard that Subhash was in Kabul he was really surprised.

He was thinking that how he could help this great revolutionary leader so as to help him escape from the British government to fulfill his mission. Uttamchand asked Bhagat Ram, "What kind of help you expect from me?"

Bhagat Ram answered, "First and foremost, arrange a safe place for us to stay. Secondly, after contacting some embassy some arrangements should be made for Subhash's departure for Moscow. Although we have established connection with Italy but Subhash Babu is not very keen to go to Berlin or Rome."

"As far as, the place of residence concerned, you can stay at my home. But in my opinion, it is not a very safe place. Secondly, the locality where I live is a very congested and shabby place. I am afraid as to how I could ask a great personality to stay there?" Uttamchand said.

Bhagat Ram laughed— "In this situation who is bothered about dirt and garbage. Secondly, compared to the inn where we are staying right now your house will be far safer and tidier. Don't worry, if Subhash Babu can stay in that dingy inn then he can stay in your house too. OK, it is getting late. I should reach Subhash Bose in time lest some problem occur. In my opinion, tonight we should stay in the inn."

Uttamchand answer — "If you were not in a hurry to change the place, then I would have searched and arranged for a more suitable alternate place. But since you want to leave the inn urgently you may come here at 4 O'clock in the evening."

Five

Uttamchand's house was situated in a congested street in the Hind Gujjar Muhalla (colony). Subhash was sitting on a chair in the small room of Uttamchand's house. Uttamchand was also on a chair near him. It seemed that Subhash was immersed in some serious thought and his brain was working hard to find solution to some grave problem. Subhash's mind gets distracted when Uttamchand asked him some question.

"In such a situation what do you want to do? Till now we have not been able to establish a connection with Russian Embassy. Such a complex situation may continue even for more days."

"I am not able to understand how we can contact the Russian Embassy. My friend had made a perfect arrangement for everything on my way to Kabul, but he did not think anything regarding what we will do after reaching Kabul. Poor Bhagatram is much ignorant as I am. My friends did not even tell him the ways and means to establish contact with Russian Embassy. In my opinion they were having the false illusion that as soon as the Russian Embassy comes to know about my presence here, they will get an aero-plane ready for me. But no such thing happened.

We made efforts in every manner but were unsuccessful in all our attempts. How do we convince them that I am Subhash? They are asking a certificate or some proof. But what we can give to them as proof? I am unable to find a way to get inside the Russian embassy. The Afghani soldiers deployed outside is not letting entry into the embassy at any cost.

In my opinion, if somehow I could talk to the Ambassador then I can convince him but I am not getting an opportunity for that even. You have been staying here for such a long time. You must be having some connection with the Russian embassy. If there is any such relation, then please make some arrangements for a single meeting with the ambassador."

Uttamchand replied— "It is true that I have been staying here since a long time. But I have never tried to establish contact with the Russian Embassy. Moreover I did not want to get myself in any political work here because Russian Embassy people are very doubtful in nature and take each and every step in very cautious and careful manner. But now I will try to establish some contact with the Russian Embassy for your sake."

Subhash said, "Although during the course of our search for the Russian Embassy, we have come across Italian Embassy. There is no much difference between Germany and Italy. As far as I feel, Italian or German Embassy people will readily agree and help me to take me to their country. But I am more interested in going to Russia if they call me and make arrangements for me."

At that moment Bhagatram entered the room. Today he had attained success in meeting the Ambassador of Italy. He gave the message of Ambassador of Italy Karuni Sahab to Subhash.

"I will send a message to Berlin and Rome today itself. I will make arrangement for passport within two-three days."

Subhash instantly gave a reply to this message— "I received your massage and was very happy to receive the message. I am really grateful for your encouragement and assistance. Please do the needful to arrange for the passport at the earliest because my long stay at the place where now I am may prove to be dangerous for me. Please do express my gratitude to the officials in Berlin and Rome for their assistance."

Uttamchand realized that Subhash was very keen to go abroad at the earliest. He asked Subhash, "You wanted to go to Russia but now since Italian Embassy is making arrangements for you, you won't be able to go to Russia."

Subhash replied— "First of all I will try to change my route by alighting in the middle of the journey. If that is not possible, I will establish contact with Russian Embassy after reaching Rome or Berlin and then make arrangements for going to Moscow."

Uttamchand was not satisfied with Subhash's answer. He further asked— "Do you think Germany or Italy will give you permission to go to Russia? I do not have any hope that in this War scenario they will so easily leave you once you are in their country."

Subhash Babu replied— "I also hold the same opinion that they won't let me go so easily. But I will make all possible efforts on my part. When I can reach Berlin from India, I can reach Moscow also from Berlin."

Preparations get started. Italian Embassy started the procedure. It made regular correspondence with Subhash and gave assurance to Subhash. One fine morning all the arrangements were made final. And the young and brave leader, with the dream of freeing India from foreign domination departed to Berlin and reached there on 28th March in a very dexterous and clandestine manner.

Six

The signs of destruction of British imperialism were becoming evident. Germany was already opposed to the British, now Japan also joined the list of opponents. Japan also took arms against British. Nature itself made arrangements to crush the ego of British.

Japan attacked England in such a manner that many of its parts came under their control. English soldiers stood helpless witnessing their defeat at the hands of Japan.

7th December 1941

Japan attacked Pearl Harbor and within the wink of eyes seized it under their control.

On 20th December 1941 the two warships of England 'Prince of Wales' and 'Ripples' got immersed in the deep oceans.

The British officers who were staying in Malaya considered them the prophets and were against the army. They did not have any sense of cooperation towards the army officials. And because of this the whereabouts of the air force was not to be found.

The result of this was that on 2nd January, Manila was defeated and in Asia not only the British Empire but the government of all Western nations faced a defeat.

Those who considered themselves to be very brave and strong backed out. The Japanese army deployed at Thailand began to move forward towards Malaya and Burma.

Japanese army was spread all over. The Fort of Singapore was considered formidable but proved to be nothing before the Japanese force.

31st January 1942

The Jahore Bridge connecting the Island of Singapore with Malaya was demolished.

On 8th February, the Japanese army attacked Singapore Island. A fierce battle ensued, but the English army could not withstand Japanese might.

On 15th February, the English army surrendered unconditionally before the Japanese.

The area with a population of 50 lakhs people comprised of 25, 000 Indian army men who were also taken capture by the Japanese army.

Seven

17th February 1942, Afternoon 2 O'clock

All the army men were ordered to assemble at the Ferror Park. From the British side there were Lt. Col. Hunt, Major Fujiwara, Col. N.L. Gill and Capt. Mohan Singh and some more Japanese and Indian army personnel were present there.

Hunt addressed the army men and said:

"From today onwards you all are war prisoners. Today on behalf of British government, I hand over you to the Japanese government. Till now as you have been obeying our orders, in the same manner you will now onwards obey the orders of Japanese government."

As soon as Hunt concluded his words Major Fujiwara stood up and said, "On behalf of Japanese government, I take command over you and I hand over you to General Officer Commanding Captain Mohan Singh. He will be fully responsible for your life and death."

The representatives from Japan put forth a plan before Indian army— "Many countries have been in the clutches of British imperialism for a long time. Japan has been fighting for the freedom of all these countries. Japan wants to establish a novel administrative system in Asia. In this new form of administration, all the countries located in East Asia would help each other for the benefit of each other. All the countries would be free and all would enjoy equal status."

"Independence of India is very essential for peace in Asia and all over the world. It is the duty of every Indian to work for the independence of the country. Japan will extend every kind of cooperation to India in its effort to attain independence."

Now it was the turn of Captain Mohan Singh. He got up and addressed the soldiers. He said, "The days of British dominance over India are coming to an end. The Japanese army has already expelled them from Singapore and Malaya. In Burma also British army is facing a very shameful defeat. India is standing on the threshold of independence. It is duty of each and every citizen of India to wipe out this evil British rule which has been sucking the blood of India for centuries. We have been dreaming of independence for such a long time. Now it is the time for dream fulfillment. And Japan has promised all sorts of support in this endeavor. Now we have to unify ourselves and fight for the sake of our 40 crores fellow countrymen."

In the end Mohan Singh revealed his actual objective— "To achieve this mission of ours we will enroll ex-soldiers from Indian army and other citizens and form an Azad Hind Fauj."

The sky reverberated with the sound of 'Inquilab Zindabad'.

Most of the Indian soldiers gave their consent to join the Azad Hind Fauj.

Captain Mohan Singh took along with him Captain Alladitta Khan and made preparations for their future plans. Their aim was to form a big army at the earliest.

Two hundred volunteers enrolled by Captain Mohan Singh went from place to place and propagated for Azad Hind Fauj and instilled the feeling of patriotism in their minds.

Captain Mohan Singh was happy and excited by the success achieved by this little effort on their part. Thirty thousand people volunteered to join the Azad Hind Fauj.

Captain Mohan Singh then decided to call a meeting of higher officials. He was of the opinion that the views of everyone should be taken into consideration to accomplish such a big task.

The commanding officer of each unit was entrusted with the task of seeking the opinion of their respective officers and had to send the same to the Head office of Captain Mohan Singh.

After the receipt of opinion from all units, in April 1942 a meeting of all the officers was called. Many arguments and counter-arguments arose in the course of the meeting. In the end the following points came to forefront:

1. We all are Indians. We do not believe in any kind of inequality based on status, caste, creed, religion or birth.

2. India's independence is our birth right.

3. An Armed Force is to be formed to fight for India's freedom.

4. This force will fight the battle only if called to do so by the Indian National Congress or the majority of Indians.

It was also decided that this decision should be circulated to each and every volunteers and those who accept the decision should be enlisted.

Eight

A mega conference of Indians, who were settled in various parts of East Asia, was held at Bangkok. Around 100 representatives from various cities took part in this conference.

A Council of Action was formulated with aim of working towards achieving India's independence.

The prominent members of the council were Sh Rasbehari Bose, Captain Mohan Singh, Sh N. Raghavan, Sh K.P. Menon and Lt. Col. G. Q. Gilani.

The Japanese government agreed to provide arms and ammunition to the Indian soldiers to fight the War of Independence. Captain Mohan Singh was informed about the proposal of provision of arms to the Indian soldiers. Captain Mohan Singh was indeed waiting for this day. And soon the formation of Azad Hind Fauj was formally announced.

On the one hand Indian soldiers were eager to join Azad Hind Fauj and on the other hand Japan was misusing this army of Indian soldiers.

From time to time Japanese officers demanded Indian soldiers for their personal errands. Some Japanese officers tried to take Indian soldiers forcefully. In such a situation coordination and maintenance of discipline among Indian soldiers became very difficult.

Col. Gill informed about this to Gen. Mohan Singh and opposed this kind of behavior on the part of Japanese Officers. Azad Hind Fauj exercised precautions according to the situation and now the supply of Indian soldiers to Japan ceased.

On 8th December 1942, the Japanese government arrested Col. Gill accusing him as a British spy. He was considered the main cause of this conflict that arose between Indian soldiers and Japanese officers.

With the arrest of Col. Gill, the officials of Azad Hind Fauj were really perturbed. The members of the Council of Action tendered their resignation. The officials felt that Japanese officials were breaking their earlier promises. So it would be better not to keep any relation with them.

The Chief of Council of Action, Sh Ras Bihari Bose asked all the branches of Azad Hind Fauj to continue with their activities. He decided to meet the Prime Minister of Japan at Tokyo. But neither General Mohan Singh nor any other members of Council of Action liked this idea.

The condition deteriorated. It was becoming clearly evident that Azad Hind Fauj requires such a strong leadership who can better and strongly coordinate the activities of the Fauj. Such a leadership who commands unquestionable authority as well as respect that the soldiers and high ranking officers become equally ready to lay down their lives.

All of them knew that there is only one person who can strongly shoulder the responsibilities of Azad Hind Fauj and that was Subhash Chandra Bose.

Nine

Efforts to bring Subhash Chandra Bose to Asia began.

The soldiers were desirous of having Subhash to boost their morale, and then they were ready to sacrifice their blood.

The World War was getting fiercer day by day.

The route from Europe to Asia was turning dangerous day by day. The English and American warships were keeping a strict vigil on the ocean route. In such a situation how was it possible to bring Subhash to Asia? The Japanese government was afraid of taking the risk of transporting Subhash to Tokyo.

Subhash was informed about the real situation. The Japanese Ambassador went and met Subhash personally at Berlin.

'Dear Subhash Sir, your life is valuable. It is very difficult to reach Tokyo without being detected by anyone. My advice to you is not to take any risk.'

Netaji Subhash replied- "I must go there. My presence there is necessary. I will undertake this journey despite every danger inherent. Even if I die on route to Tokyo I will be happy and satisfied that I lost my life in the process of fighting for the motherland. I welcome such a death."

3rd June 1943

Sh. Ras Bihari Bose departed to Tokyo to welcome Netaji. His arrival was kept a secret.

20th June 1943

Subhash Babu reached Tokyo in a ship. He was accompanied by his A.D.C Abid Ali Hasan.

At Tokyo Subhash received a warm welcome. General Tejo himself was present there to receive him. Many people from various places of East Asia had arrived in Tokyo to welcome Subhash.

In fact, Subhash was extended the sort of welcome befitting to a revolutionary who had defeated the British Empire.

After reaching Tokyo, in a statement, Subhash said, "During this World War the British policymakers had befooled our leader. Hence now we have firmly decided that we will not trust them anymore.

British imperialism had its negative impact on India causing moral degradation, destruction of culture, economic downfall and political dependence. It is our duty to pay the debt of independence with our blood.

We will be compelled to safeguard our freedom we have gained after so much of sacrifice with all our strength. We will attain our independence after undergoing so many hardships."

22nd June 1943

To continue with India's efforts of attaining freedom, Subhash Babu put forth the proposal of setting up an army of Indians in East Asia and requested the public to extend help and cooperation in this work.

Netaji said, "The responsibility of breaking the shackles of foreign rule in India lies with the Indians. We cannot leave this responsibility on anyone else. It will be against our national honor.

But our enemy is well equipped with arms and ammunitions. In front of such a powerful enemy 'Satyagraha' might be a failure. Hence if we want to expel British power from our country, we should fight them with their own arms.

The enemy has taken out the sword, so we should also use the sword power to fight against them.

I am sure that with the help of Indians settled in East Asia, I will be able to build such a powerful force, which will root out British rule from India. The auspicious time has come. Every Indian should go the battle field. When the blood of freedom loving Indians will drop on the earth, then only will India attain independence."

2nd July 1943

Subhash had made all preparations for going to Singapore. Only officials of Azad Hind Fauj were informed about his Singapore visit.

Many Indians, Japanese Ambassadors, Army staff and higher officials of Azad Hind Fauj assembled at the airport to welcome Subhash Babu.

A special force comprising of chosen soldiers from Azad Hind Fauj was formed to salute Subhash.

At around 11 am, a Japanese aircraft landed at the airport. Every moment that they spent waiting for their beloved leader seemed heavy. Everybody had just one mission in their minds to have a glance of their beloved leader. Each one of them desired to touch his feet with their heads out of reverence. All of them wanted to sacrifice everything they had in front of that great patriot.

The door of the aeroplane opened and Subhash alighted from it along with his companion Abid Hussain. The crowd began to hail their great leader. The soldiers saluted him and stood awe inspired by his personality.

4th July 1943

'Indian Freedom Conference' was held at Singapore. A huge meeting was held at Cathay House. The place was thronged by crowds of people. After a historic speech, Sh.Rasbihari Bose handed over the girdles of freedom movement to Subhash Chandra Bose.

Netaji accepted this big responsibility and said, "Friends, the time is ripe to use armed force to attain freedom. To fulfill our objective of complete freedom we need the services of soldiers as well as dedication towards our motherland. I request my countrymen to get united under one flag. This step on your part has not only the support of our nationalist leaders but also one fourth population is in our support. This is for the first time in the history of the world that Indians settled abroad are also supporting the cause of freedom.

Some of our friends think that Britain will accept our demand for freedom in the current circumstances. But all these hopes have proved to be mere dreams. This shows that Britain is all bent on exploiting India to maximum possible level."

Reminding the history of Indian Freedom Movement, Subhash Babu said— "Any kind of treaty with Britain would prove to be harmful for us. It will harm our interests. The world history is a witness to the fact that no battle for freedom can be successful without the help of outside forces."

In this context he further said, "Japan is the only country which has been able to put up a strong opposition against Western forces. It is the heartfelt desire of Japan to free Asian countries. Now we have got a golden opportunity to attain freedom and now we will lay the foundation for a new world order based on truth, justice and freedom.

Now I want to talk to people who have doubts about my capability and integrity. I promise that I will always remain dedicated to my country. I can never ditch my motherland. I will live for my country and die for it. There is no one who can lead me astray from the correct path.

Every Indian should understand that the victory of Britain is the defeat of India. Circumstances and time are in our favor. If we are ready to fight and lay down our lives then we are sure to attain freedom. We will get our freedom at the cost of our blood. And with this we will be able to lay the foundation of national unity and integrity. We will be capable of protecting our freedom so achieved in a much better manner."

In the end Subhash clarified:

"Although we have complete faith in our final victory, still we should not underestimate the power of our enemy. We should face and overcome all these hurdles that come in our way with all might and bravery. Our enemy is not only powerful and brave but also unkind and cruel. We should be well prepared to face all hardships during the course of this war. You will attain independence only when you are able to prove yourself in this acid test. I am sure that you will achieve your objective and will lead this poor and down trodden country towards the path of prosperity. Long live our freed nation."

This passionate speech by Subhash Bose entered the very soul of the crowd present there. His words had a magical appeal. Renunciation, prayer and sacrifice -- the three principles which Subhash had imbibed in his life served as source of inspiration to all those present there. His speech was so meaningful and rationale that his opponents also got attracted towards it.

The very presence of such an exuberant and youthful leader in the midst of those Indians who lived away from their soil in East Asia was a sort of wish fulfillment for them.

The whole atmosphere echoed with thunderous applause and hailing of Netaji.

5th July 1943

The most historical declaration in the direction of India's independence was made on that day—the formal establishment of Azad Hind Fauj. A parade of all the platoons of Azad Hind Fauj was organized in front of Municipal Bhawan, Singapore. Netaji inspected the army and later on addressing the soldiers he said:-

"Dear Soldiers of India's Freedom Movement! Today is the most honorable moment of my life. With God's blessings I have got this fortune and honor to declare to the whole world that the soldiers who will pave the way for India's independence is ready. This force has, after its organization, gone to Singapore, which was once the fort of British Imperialism. This is the army, which will not only wipe out British force from India but will also lay the foundation of the construction of the national army once India becomes free. Every Indian should feel proud that this army has been formed completely under the leadership of Indians and when the historic moment will arrive then it will be out on the battle field.

There was a time when people thought that the Sun the British Empire will never set, it is eternal. But I was never ever bothered about such a thought. History has taught me that every empire faces downfall at one point of time or the other. In addition, I have seen with my eyes those cities and forts which were the landmarks of those past empires which have now turned into burial ground. Here standing on the burial ground of British empire, even a child can believe that the glory of British Empire is a thing of the past."

On the occasion, coining the slogan, 'Delhi Chalo' (Go to Delhi), Subhash declared—

"In 1939 when France declared war against Germany, only one slogan came out from the mouths of German soldiers, 'Move to Paris' (Paris Chalo). When the brave Japanese soldiers took up the decision to attack the Western world in December 1941, they had only one voice—'Singapore Chalo' (Move to Singapore). Dear friends, soldiers, our war slogan is 'Delhi Chalo'. I do not know how many of us will remain safe and alive in this war of independence but I am sure that in the end victory will be ours and our work will not end till that time when our brave soldiers who have had survived the war carry out a victory march at Red Fort, the burial ground of British glory.

In my whole of public life, I have always experienced that though India is ready by all means to attain freedom, still it is facing some kind of shortage and that is a proper, well-organized army."

In this contest, citing the examples of America and Italy he said, "George Washington of America fought for freedom and won the battle for freedom because he had a well-organized army with him. Garibaldi could free Italy because he had armed volunteers for his help. It is your good fortune that Indians themselves came forward to build a national army for India. By doing so, we have overcome the last possible obstruction that might have come in our way of freedom. It is a matter of pleasure and glory that Indians are the pioneers and path breakers in this significant work."

Continuing with his speech he said, "You have dual responsibilities to fulfill. With armed force and your blood you have to attain freedom. After that when India attains freedom, and then you have to form an independent army whose work will be to safeguard India's freedom and sovereignty. We should establish such a strong foundation of national security that in future we should not lose our freedom at any cost."

Enumerating the responsibilities of the soldiers he said, "As a soldier, you should always follow the three principles i.e., dedication, integrity and sacrifice. Those soldiers who are always ready to lay down their lives for the sake of patriotism, they always emerge victorious. If you also want to become invincible then let these three ideals get embedded in your heart."

Subhash drew attention to the duties and responsibilities of army officers and said— "Those who are officers, I want to tell them that they have heavy responsibilities on their shoulders. Though every army officer has a very significant role to play, your role is even more significant. Because of your political history, we do not have any inspirational stories in front of us. We should forget many things that British had taught us and learn many things that they have not taught. Still I am sure that the responsibilities your countrymen have handed over to you, you will accomplish them very well. Always remember, the officers either construct the army or become instrumental in their destruction. Also remember that it was due to weak leadership that British army faced defeats at many fronts and you should be instrumental in formation of a higher quality of army for the Azad Hind Fauj.

Dear friends, you have chosen a very noble profession. To achieve such an objective any sacrifice, not even sacrificing your life, is insufficient. You are the guards of India's pride and the lively depiction of India's ambition and hopes. Hence behave in such a manner that your fellow countrymen bless you and future generation remembers you."

In the end, Subhash assured all of them and said, "I assure you all that in darkness, in light, in sorrow, in joy, in sufferings and in victory— always I will be with you. At this moment I cannot give you anything other than hunger, thirst, difficulties, compelled battle and death. But you support me in life and death, as I believe that you will surely do, and then I can lead you to victory and freedom. It is not important that how many of us will be alive to see independent India, but it is sufficient that India will be free from foreign domination and to free it will forfeit everything."

26th August 1943

Netaji took over the command of Azad Hind Fauj and issued an important dossier in this regard—

"For the benefit of India's Freedom Movement I have took over the command of Azad Hind Fauz. This is a matter of utter pleasure and honor for me, because for any Indian, no other thing could be a cause of pride than this responsibility of holding the command of Indian National Army. I am well aware and cautious of the importance of my task. My prayer to the Almighty is to give me strength in face of adversities and fulfill my duties towards my countrymen.

I consider myself to be the servant of 38 crores Indians. I have decided to fulfill my duties in such a manner that I am able to safeguard the interest of whole of the 38-crore population and every Indian have complete faith in me. The Indian National Army can be made only on the foundation of true patriotism, complete justice and total equality.

In the forthcoming battle for freedom and for the formation of a truly Indian government of independent India, the role of Azad Hind Fauj is very significant. To accomplish this task we should be united as one army, the sole objective of which would be the freedom of our country and whose sole desire would be either independence or death. When Azad Hind Fauj will enter into the battle field it would be like a wall made of marble invincible and when it will attack its opponent it will be like a steam roller just unstoppable.

Our task is not an easy one. The battle would be long and difficult but we have full faith in our mission and our indomitability. It is the right of these 38 crores people, the one fifth of world population to attain freedom. Now they are prepared to give up their lives. Hence there is not a single force on this earth that can stop us from achieving our birth right.

Friends, with your unconditional support and your true dedication Azad Hind Fauj will become instrumental in achieving freedom for India. I assure you all that in the end victory will be ours. We should continue with our slogan 'Delhi Chalo' till our national flag is hoisted over the Viceroy's House in New Delhi and Azad Hind Fauj march victoriously inside the Red Fort."

21st October 1943

The Historical meeting of Indian freedom League was held at Cathay Bhawan. All the representatives from East Asian Countries attended the meeting.

Sh. Ras Bihari Bose read the welcome speech and Col. Chatterjee read out the Report of the Secretariat.

That day the temporary Azad Hind Government was established. Netaji took oath for assuring complete dedication towards India. The huge hall reverberated with sounds of applause and cheers.

Netaji was becoming so emotional that his voice choked. He was so overcome with emotions that he could not speak any more. It proved that every word spoken by him was coming out from his inner soul.

Subhash taking great efforts in controlling his emotions, trying to up and low his tone, but in a powerful voice said, "With Lord Almighty as I witness, I am taking this pious oath that, I Subhash Bose, in order to free India and 38 crores of its population, will continue with this struggle for freedom till the end of my life."

Saying this much he stopped. It seemed as if he will break down. Those present there were also repeating these words.

The Hall had turned peaceful. Tears came in the eyes of people present there. Still people controlled their emotions.

Then Subhash continued in a serious tone— "I will always remain be a servant of my country and safe guard the interests of its population. This will be my greatest responsibility.

Even after gaining freedom I will be ready to shed my last drop of blood for saving the interests of my nation."

After that, each member of the temporary government took oath personally. Netaji Subhash Bose read out the main manifesto of Azad Hind Government.

"In 1857, after facing defeat for the first time at the hands of British in Bengal, the people of India have been fighting fiercely and tough battles for so many years. The history of those days is filled with instances of incomparable bravery and self sacrifice. The pages of history are filled with tales of courage and velour of Siraj-ud-daullah and Mohan Lal of Bengal; Haider Ali, Tipu Sultan and Velu Tampi of South India, Appa Sahab Bhonsle and Peshwa Baji Rao from Maharashtra, Begums from Awadh, Sardar Shyam Singh Atariwala from Punjab, Rani Laxmi Bai and Tantia Tope from North, Maharaja Kunwar Singh and Nana Saheb Peshwa from Dumrao, written in golden words. Unfortunately our forefathers could not foresee the dangers of British rule. Hence they did not fight the British force in a united manner. In the end when Indians actually realized the situation, they united against British and fought against them under the flagship of Bahadurshah Zafar in 1857.

The British rule in India drained off India's wealth leading it to hunger and poverty deaths. Gradually Indians began to develop a sense of distrust towards British. They just required a small flame to fire their desire for breaking the shackles of British domination. The duty of Indian National Army is to fire this flame.

Since the dawn of freedom is near us, it is our responsibility to form a permanent government and began our last conflict under its leadership. Since almost all of our leaders are in prison and Indians are totally unarmed, it is the duty of the Indian Freedom Union formed by the East Asian Indians to form a temporary Azad Hind Government.

The demand of this temporary government is unquestionable obedience of all its members. In turn it assures all the citizens' religious freedom and equality.

In the name of god and in the name of those brave soldiers who laid down their lives for India and left behind examples of sacrifice and courage, I call all the people to assemble under our flag and fight for our freedom. I call all of you to oppose British and their Indian supporters. I call upon you to continue this struggle till India gains complete independence."

The manifests depicted a clear picture of the principles and philosophy of Azad Hind Government.

Those present there were pleased and accepted the formation of temporary Azad Hind government. All of them promised to fight for freedom till the last drop of blood is drained from their body. Officials of the Azad Hind Government were also nominated.

Chief of the Government, Prime Minister, Foreign and Defense Minister — Subhash Chandra Bose

President of Women Union — Captain Lakshmi

Publication and Broadcasting — M.A. Aiyyar

Finance — Lt. Col. A.C. Chatterjee

Representatives of Armed Forces — Lt. Col Gulzar Singh, Lt. Col. N.S. Bhagat, Lt. Col. J.K. Bhonde, Lt. Col M. L. Kiyani, Lt. Col. A.D. Loknathan, Lt. Col. Ahsan Qadir, Lt. Col. Shahnawaz

Chief Advisor — Ras Bihari Bose

Advisors — Karimgani, Devnath Das, D.M. Khan

Legal Advisor — A.N. Sarkar

Ten

22nd October 1943

This is the birthday of Rani Jhansi and on this day 'Rani Jhansi Regiment' was formed unfurling the national flag. The newly formed all women force was ready carrying rifles. Subhash inaugurated the Rani Jhansi Training Centre. A significant task was getting accomplished.

Mothers are the ones who inspire their sons to sacrifice their lives for the sake of the country. And when their blood gets heated up what's not they can do?

Subhash was well aware of such a situation. In his passionate speech, addressing the females he said, "Our past is great and glorious and without such a glorious tradition a brave woman like Rani Jhansi could not have taken birth in this country. There are many examples before us right from ancient times to the present which have been a source of inspiration for us. Ahalya Bai, Rani Bhawani of Bengal, Razia Begum, Noor Jahan were the great administrators who ruled India before the British domination. I have full faith in the power of fertility of Indian soil and I am sure that as in the past a powerful women's group will be formed in the future.

Rani Jhansi fought the battle against British at a young age of 20 years. You all must be well aware about the intention of a young girl of 20 riding on the horse and fighting with swords in the battle field. You can imagine the great strength and courage inherent in that young woman.

One English commander fighting against the force of Rani Jhansi had said that, "She was the bravest of all the soldiers."

In the end Subhash said— "Unfortunately Rani of Jhansi was defeated in the battle. It was not her defeat. In fact she accepted death and her soul will remain alive forever.

India can give birth to many more such Ranis of Jhansi. I know many of you have the capability and capacity that Rani of Jhansi possessed.

I request you all to get ready once again and then you will see that we all are breathing the air of independent India."

The hearts of innumerable women longed to lay down their lives for the sake of the nation after hearing such an inspirational speech by Netaji and they immediately volunteered for the cause. The Rani Jhansi regiment was formally established and Dr. Lakshmi Swaminathan was appointed the Commander of the Regiment.

25th October 1943

The temporary Azad Hind Government declared war against Britain and United States.

A mass meeting of Indians and Indian National Army was organized in front of Municipal Bhawan in Singapore.

The Council of Ministers, in this meeting, passed a proposal—'Temporary Azad Hind Government declares a war against Britain and United States.'

This long awaited declaration raised cheers among the crowd that echoed the sky. For almost 15 minutes chaos and confusion prevailed over the around 50,000 people present there. Many of them tried to reach the stage.

After much effort the people were controlled and calmed down.

At that moment Netaji said, "All of you can stand up at your respective places and express your support for the proposal by raising your hands."

All around one could see only hands raised in the air. Perhaps there was hardly anyone who had not raised his hand.

The soldiers raised their rifles and kept them on their shoulders to express support for the proposal.

Some females of Rani Jhansi Regiment fell unconscious due to excitement. Many of them, in a state of stupor kept on repeating the slogan 'Delhi Chalo.'

On 28 October 1943, Netaji spoke on the occasion of a Press Meet of journalists from all over the world.

"With the formation of a temporary Azad Hind

Government, I have fulfilled my second dream of my political life. My first dream was the formation of a revolutionary army. One more dream remains to be fulfilled and that is the battle for freedom and attainment of independence.

The world knows that nationalist India has been fighting with British since a long period. When we have already formed the temporary government, we should present our views before Britain and America.

Our war declaration is not mere propaganda. We will prove that we transform our speech into action. I never decide anything, unless I am confident of accomplishing it."

8th November 1943

Japanese government handed over the Andaman Nicobar islands to the temporary government of Azad Hind.

Subhash Bose issued a statement at that moment in which he stated – "Independence of Andaman has its symbolic significance because the British have always been using Andaman as a political prison. Many revolutionaries, who opposed British rule, laid their lives here and many were imprisoned in this island. This very Andaman attained independence in the first instance of freedom struggle. Here many patriots have suffered torture and torment. Slowly and gradually Indian boundaries will attain freedom but Andaman Islands have its historic significance. In the name of war heroes I rechristen the name of Andaman as '*Shahid*' and Nicobar as '*Swaraj*'."

19th November 1943

The first battalion of Subhash Brigade Regiment completed its training. It was fully armed with necessary arms and ammunitions and the battalion was send to Rangoon through rail route.

A heart rending scene ensued at the station. Those soldiers who were detained by doctors at Taipei due to weakness and ill-health, all of them laid down on the railway tracks.

They said, "We should be given permission to join the battle. We had taken oath before Netaji. We want to self-sacrifice ourselves for our nation. Then why are we being detained here? Why we are denied of our rights?"

When they were promised that they will be sent along with other troops then only they got up from the tracks. The last troop left the place by 24 November. The troops travelled continuously for five weeks. In addition to train they had to travel on foot for about 400 miles.

The soldiers did not have a proper means of transportation, no proper woolen clothes to fight cold weather conditions, nor any emergency provisions. Nevertheless they all were elated and excited. They were well aware that in this battle they will achieve nothing but hardships and death but they were true patriots who were not perturbed by such thoughts. They were ready to accept death at any cause and that too gladly. The troops marched forward towards Rangoon. By the beginning of January 1944 a big part of the Regiment reached Rangoon.

4th January 1944

Netaji Subhash Bose reached Rangoon in a Japanese aircraft. There he set up his office to accomplish his future tasks.

He felt that they are falling short of time to begin an attack on their enemies. He began to make preparations to send the soldiers to the battle field and he himself inspected the minute details in this regard. Many hardships cropped up on the process but he faced all of them strongly. The soldiers lack some essential provisions necessary for the battle but seeing the excitement of the soldiers, Subhash pacified himself. Whatever arrangements they could make in a hurried manner, they just did that.

7th January 1944

In Burma, Subhash met Japanese Commander-in-Chief General Kababe. General Shahnawaz was also with him. In the meeting they discussed regarding the modus operandi of the battle to be fought by Azad Hind Fauj and the support they are likely to get from Japanese Army.

General Kababe said, "In my opinion, it would not be right. By doing so, the troops will lose their existence. I won't accept this. Azad Hind Fauj will not be broken into small pieces and it will have Indian officials supervising it." He further said, "Our army will extend complete cooperation to Indian soldiers. They will lead you."

Netaji said, "No, the independence we gain with the sacrifice of Japanese soldiers would be worse than dependence. Hence for the glory of India it is necessary that Indians themselves sacrifice their lives. I want that the first drop of blood that soak the Indian soil should be that of the soldier of Azad Hind Fauj.

Netaji discussed many other things also with the Japanese Commander-in-Chief. General assured help and support in other forms to the Indian soldiers.

Subhash spent all his time in all round preparations and inspired the citizens of Burma. Many rich patriots helped Subhash Babu with donations in lakhs. In the meantime the office of Azad Hind Fauj was also set up in Burma.

24th January 1944

Japanese Commander-in-Chief, the Chief of the General Staff, General Katakura visited Netaji. He handed over the detailed report of the activities till that date to Netaji. He also briefed about the strategies to be followed while attacking the British army at the Indo-Burmese Border.

The meeting was kept a total secret. Only the three were present -- Netaji, General Katakura and General Shahnawaz.

General Katakura said, "In order to intimidate British it is essential to unleash an attack on them at a great speed. For this, we feel that, Calcutta should be made a target for dropping bombs."

Netaji opposed this and said, "I don't want to destroy my

beautiful city with bombs. Moreover, in my opinion, it is not a good idea to drop bombs where people reside. If I do so, Indians will lose their faith on me."

Netaji handed over the Subhash Brigade to the Japanese Headquarter at Burma with a view to get them prepared for the battle field.

3rd February 1944

Netaji gave the valedictory speech. His speech that instilled patriotic fervor in the minds of the soldiers was indeed very surprising. Around 3000 soldiers stood still listening to his speech for over one and half hours.

Netaji said, "My dear friends! You are the strength of my arms. With your strength I will safeguard the rights of India. In the battlefield, your action will matter the most and decide our future."

He warned— "The first big force of Azad Hind Fauj is on the battle field. Japanese will try and test you in all possible ways. Hence those who are afraid of death should stay back."

The face of the soldiers turned red with excitement. All of them said in a singular voice—'We all will go for the war.'

Not a single soldier came forward to stay back. Nobody was afraid of death. All of them assured that they will never defame the Indian glory by running away from the battle field.

Eleven

By 4th and 5th February 1944, the first, second and third battalions of the Brigade departed for Prome and Mandley.

Major Mehmood Ahmed and Major Ram Swaroop left for Rangoon on 5 February 1944 in a motorcar. On 8 February they reached Mandley.

On 10th February General Shahnawaz Khan, went to North Burma to meet all the Japanese Commanders.

The first regiment was entrusted the task of taking position at Haka-Falm. By 12th February almost all the soldiers of second and third Batallion reached Mandley.

Around 300 soldiers of Azad Hind Fauj departed from Mandley to Kaleba. Along with Japanese soldiers, brave soldiers chosen from Azad Hind Fauj were deployed at sensitive locations.

They were not bothered about their comforts but were swayed by the feeling of patriotism and were longing for attaining freedom for their country. In the most harsh circumstances, without thinking about hunger, ill-health, the soldiers were keen to fulfill their duties.

A fierce battle ensued. Slowly the brave soldiers began to consolidate power at various positions.

On 18th March 1944 Azad Hind Fauj crossed the border connecting India and Burma and stepped on to its pious motherland. All the soldiers were joyous to experience that moment.

Soon they took over Kohima also. On 19th March Lt. Sikander Khan in a combat attack took control over Phalam.

On the meantime, the Rani Jhansi Regiment organized a meeting. The female team of soldiers was also anxious to be on the battle front.

A request letter was sent to Netaji in which all of them signed with their blood.

They said that they too have taken an oath to lay down their lives for the motherland. 'We were assured that we will be sent to the battle front, hence it is our request to permit us to join the battle.'

On 22nd March 1944 Rani Jhansi Regiment was granted permission to the war front. Netaji did not think that repressing their excitement will be of any good.

April 1944

The female soldiers of the Rani Jhansi Regiment marched ahead towards the battle field. Forests and hills were no obstruction for them.

The inhabitants of different villages were surprised to see their patriotic fervor. They had never imagined of a female army.

They crossed fences and hills, taking routes embedded with pebbles and stones. They got themselves settled on a valley.

One day they felt that the British army was there at a distance of one mile.

The British army was caught unaware. They could not have imagined the presence of an exclusive female army at that place, even in the wildest of their dreams. No sooner than the British army reached there, the Rani Jhansi Regiment began firing.

The British army was taken aback.

'Inquilab Zindabad', 'Azad Hind Zindabad', 'Jai Hind', 'Dilli Chalo' reverberated all around the hills and valleys. In the first attack itself the British army tasted the bitter taste of defeat. For over 16 hours they fought the British army. Once again women proved their mettle over men.

The war was getting fiercer. The soldiers of Azad Hind Fauj faced their powerful enemy bravely in spite of difficult situations.

At many a places the soldiers did not get anything to eat. But they were happy to eat even boiled wild grass. They ate it like a delicious meal.

At many places, they did not get that even. The provision of medicines exhausted. The soldiers protracted Beri Beri and other such diseases. But in emergency situations they forgot about their problems and sorrows.

Subhash closely perceived the situation for two months. He did not leave any stone unturned in accumulating the necessary provisions. But Japanese did not provide them with complete cooperation.

Still the soldiers were excited. Even the name of Subhash cast a magic spell over them and they forgot everything.

On 2nd July Subhash reached Rangoon.

4th July 1944

Netaji week began. One year ago, on this very day Netaji took over the reign of nationalist movements in East Asia. In the current year, on the very same day around 30 lakhs Indian stood behind Subhash in his support. On this day they took an oath—either freedom or a death.

The hall was crowded with audience. Loud speakers were set up outside on roads also. One could find only heads of people all around. Everyone was excited.

Describing the developments of the past 12 months Netaji said, "At some point of time people had their doubts as to whether Azad Hind Fauj will fight the battle or not and if at all it fights will it be able to defeat its enemy! We have passed the acid test and in fact we have got a boost to our confidence."

Till now our soldiers have not complained about any of the hardships they have been suffering in the course of the war. In fact they have complained that they were not given an opportunity to be in the war front. People listened to Netaji's speech in an utter sense of fascination and stupor. People were really excited and the crowd got dispersed after almost one and a half hours.

5th July 1944

A parade of Azad Hind Fauj was organized in Rangoon and Subhash Bose took the salute.

On the occasion Subhash Babu said, "Our enemy is worried at the formation of Azad Hind Fauj. For some time they just overlooked our very existence.

Radio Station Delhi has been broadcasting false news. It was spreading the news that war prisoners who have been made captive by Japanese are being compelled to join the Azad Hind Fauj. But a common thinking person can very well understand that with undue pressure a normal army can be constructed but not this kind of an obedient army. You can of course compel a person to take up the rifle but you cannot compel a person to give up his life for an objective which he does not consider of any value for him.

Azad Hind Fauj is an army of ex-soldiers and patriotic citizens. I want to inform you that it not only consists of male members but also female members.

Friends, Azad Hind Fauj is not only an assembly of Indians but also is imparting training by the Indians. The soldiers are fighting the battle under the command of Indian officers. This army is making efforts to attain freedom. We are waiting for that glorious day and we are shedding our blood and sweat for that day."

The soldiers took their rifles and kept them on their shoulders.

Sounds of 'Delhi Chalo' and 'Jai Hind' echoed the whole atmosphere.

Subhash praised the bravery showed by the soldiers at Arakan and gave them the medals of 'Vir Hind' and 'Sardar-e-Jung'.

6th July 1944

Subhash Babu gave a speech addressing Mahatma Gandhi which was broadcasted in the radio:

'It is futile to differentiate between British citizens and British government. Both of them are hard core imperialists. I cannot be fooled by politicians from Britain. British are the most cunning and scheming people of the world. The armed struggle will continue till that day when each Britisher is not weeded out from Indian soil and our national flag is not hoisted on the top of the Viceroy House.

Father of the nation! In this struggle for freedom we want to have your blessings.'

9th July 1944

One Muslim donated his jewelry, property and one crore rupees for the cause of freedom struggle.

10th July 1944

Subhash Babu addressed a gathering of over 30,000 people at a public function. All stood spell bound hearing his speech.

Talking about the plans of this movement he said — "Brothers, we know that as long as outside attack is not made on British army it will keep on repressing revolutionary movements. Hence Azad Hind Fauj has started this battle.

Friends! Our enemy is quite powerful. We have faced them at various occasions. Though they have enough provisions of ration and other necessary articles, still we have defeated them at many places because we have before us the question of our feelings and emotions.

In every places of the world, revolutionary army had to fight a battle similar to ours, in the same conditions, but in the end they have attained victory also. These revolutionaries do not gain their strength from liquor or meat but from trust, sacrifice, bravery and perseverance.

Azad Hind Fauj has also been taught to fight in adverse situations. It is fighting for the freedom of 38 crores of Indian population."

11th July 1944

At Rangoon, near the tomb of Bahadur Shah Zafar, the soldiers organized a march. Encouraging the soldiers Subhash said— "We should avenge the torture and torment by the British in 1857 and after that. Indians love their country but they do not know how to hate their enemies. We with teach them to do so. With the blood of our enemy we will subdue our anger and rebellion.

For this we will have to donate blood. We will wash our sins with our blood and attain our freedom thereby taking revenge against our enemies."

22nd September 1944

The death anniversary of Shahid Yatindradas was organized in Rangoon. The Jubilee Hall in Rangoon was filled with people. Speeches were given in memory of the martyrs. The story of brave Yatindradas who sacrificed his life for the sake of motherland at the Lahore Jail was retold at the occasion. The audience turned emotional hearing the heart rending story of Yatindradas.

Netaji also gave a touching speech. He gave an inspiring speech calling the people to sacrifice everything for the sake of the nation. "Nothing can stop India from gaining freedom. But this freedom struggle requires sacrifice. It requires all your strength, your wealth and everything in your possession. Renounce everything like your comforts, materialistic possessions and wealth and be like a revolutionary.

You people have given away your sons to the battle field but the goddess of freedom is not appeased by that. It needs such self-sacrificing men and women who would lay down their lives, embrace death happily and immerse the enemy in the river of their blood. ***You give me blood and I will give you freedom.***

This is the demand of freedom."

"We are ready, take our blood." Voices echoes inside the hall.

Netaji turned serious. He said, "Brothers, I do not want to sway you away by emotions. I want to bring out the rebel inside you who is ready to stake your lives."

"We are ready." Again echoes the voices. "But the contract of accepting death cannot be written with any simple ink. You will have to write it in blood. Those who can do so can come forward. I want to get your blood stamped for the sake of freedom in front of my eyes."

It seemed as if Netaji was roaring out calling for the rebels. His voice was strong in front of which even the mountains would have lowered their heads in reverence.

'We will give our blood.'

'We will lay down our lives for the country.'

'We will renounce everything.'

'We will fight till the last drop of our blood gets drained.'

Mixed voices filled the hall. The whole public inside the hall stood as if on one foot.

The women were the first ones to encircle the stage. Each wanted to be the first to sign the contract. A kind of competition prevailed over there. This contract embracing death in exchange of freedom was signed by almost everyone and the whole proceeding went on for over an hour.

What an indescribable scene. The glory of our ancient history once again got refreshed in their memories.

Twelve

Three platoons were formed to attack Imphal. In spite of adverse conditions, the Azad Hind Fauj put up a brave fight against its enemy in this sector. It wiped out the enemies and hoisted the tricolor.

The forest area of Imphal was completely surrounded and the transportation and communication facilities of the cities were cut off. The soldiers were not getting enough food and other provisions but they possessed a strange kind of excitement. They were ready to face any kind of hardships.

Suddenly Japan stopped providing aerial assistance. But the soldiers were fully aware of their duties and responsibilities. They continued with the attack. Their continuous attack compelled the British army to turn back.

One day, Indian soldiers were fighting a fierce battle. The British army was facing a complete defeat. They were running towards Dhimapur but Indian soldiers closed the Kohima road. They wanted to trap the British soldiers and make them captive.

The British soldiers were in a trapped situation. They didn't have any other alternative. Either they have to accept defeat unconditionally or continue fighting back. Quickly they circled the Indians soldiers with their motors and tanks. It became impossible for the Indian soldiers to break this trap. Without the help of air-force it was impossible for Indian soldiers to counter attack but the Japanese had already suspended all their air-force help. The situation had become quite alarming and dangerous.

On the one hand they had to stop the attack of their enemies and on the other they were running short of provisions. But they bravely continued with their combat and they were really hopeful of their victory.

But godly wrath! Rains began before one month than usual. All transport connections were cut off. The supply of provisions for Indian soldiers stopped. Still Indian soldiers did not lose heart. They continued fighting.

But this time bombs and shells fell short. Rifles, guns and pistols proved useless. Machine guns also became dysfunctional.

The British soldiers installed 12 canons on the hills but Azad Hind Fauj has only one. But the blood of the Indian soldiers was boiling for freedom. The veins were hungry; the intestines dry, lips turned black with hunger but the lovers of freedom were fighting for their freedom with hungry stomach.

The officers were worried. One day in the evening one soldier came running by. He was palpitating, his throat had turned dry. He shouted eagerly, "Brothers! Our officer is planning to take us back from the battle field."

The soldiers were worried, eyes turned red, they were angry. "Impossible! We have to reach Delhi. Netaji has said 'Even if you have to die, you should not turn back!' We won't deceive our Netaji. Even after death we won't turn our backs!"

Soldiers were perturbed. The officials understood the situation and tried to make the soldiers understand the situation.

The officer said, "We do not have proper means of transportation."

"We will walk on foot. We will pull the canon with one hand and carry the provisions on our back. We will shoulder the weight of freedom."

"We do not have any weapons."

"We will sacrifice every drop of our blood. Nobody has snatched away our courage from us."

"We have neither medicines nor medical facilities."

"Our wounds will be our source of inspiration. And our pain will be our medicine."

"We do not have a grain to eat."

"We will stay alive by eating leaves. We will fight empty stomach. It is Netaji's order."

The officials were left without any words. The soldiers were strong in their decision. It was impossible to convince them anymore.

The danger for Indian soldiers was looming large. Their lives were in danger.

Somehow Subhash was informed about the situation. Subhash sent his message.

The next day the soldiers were called back.

The soldiers were disappointed by the orders of Subhash. Tears came rolling down their eyes. These are the tears of disappointment.

Imphal could not be conquered.

11th October 1944

Netaji departed for Rangoon. He had come for the inspection of the front platoons. He was sorrowed to see the situation.

He called the meeting of Cabinet Ministers in Rangoon. Netaji presented the report on the war and the reasons for the defeat in Imphal.

Once again they began to gather provisions for the war. In order to speed up the war process, recruitments of soldiers in Azad Hind Fauj began at a mass scale.

Now the number of soldiers in Azad Hind Fauj reached to 50,000. Subhash ordered the soldiers to reach Minmana.

By the end of January 1945 the women division and Moniva hospital were removed and a new Division Camp was established in Minmana.

18th February 1945

Netaji reached Minmana to inspect the new division of the army. He saw that the officers and soldiers of the first division were more unwell. Only 20 per cent of them were having arms in their possession.

At that moment they received information that in the nearby warfront the Nehru Brigade is indulged in a fight with the enemy and there were heavy casualties on the Indian side.

The enemy was making efforts to reach Miktila. They wanted to capture the Railway Station there. With the capture of the Railway Station the Japanese soldiers deployed in Burma would have proved useless.

Subhash Babu was requested to leave Miktila at the earliest as it was felt that his valuable life was in danger. All his well wishers and army officers requested him to leave.

General Shahnawaz said, "Netaji you are putting your life in danger merely to show your courage. But you have no right to do so. Your life is a valuable heritage of mother India and I have been entrusted with the task of safeguarding it. I want to ensure that this heritage of our motherland does not go waste. If something happens to you what will happen to our freedom movement?"

Subhash Babu listened to General very carefully. A smile came over his face. He said, "Shahnawaz, it is useless to argue with me. I have decided to go to Popa and I will definitely go there. You need not worry about my safety because I knew that England has not been able to make that bomb till now that can kill Subhash."

Suddenly loud sound emanated from the sky and the enemies' aircraft began to drop bomb. Scenes of mass destruction could be witnessed all over but Subhash escaped without even any damage to his hair.

23rd February 1945

Subhash Babu reached the capital of Shaun, Tunki.

The war had become even more dangerous and destructive. The friendly countries of the enemy were constantly marching ahead. Still the soldiers of Azad Hind Fauj did not lose their hearts.

The enemies were attaining one victory after another. On the Western front Germany was facing defeat after defeat and in the East the condition of Japan was becoming precarious. Japanese were flushed out from every corner.

4th March 1945

British aircrafts kept on raining bombs continuously for hours together. Japanese were greatly frightened by this.

Though Azad Hind Fauz was trying to keep the enemy soldiers away from entering Burma, but it has limited resources to continue with its efforts. In such a situation, they were unable to do anything further.

The enemy was attaining continuous victory and was marching ahead towards Burma.

Subhash was greatly angered by the defeat of Azad Hind Fauj. The streaks of worry were quite evident on his face.

The major issue before him was to safeguard Rangoon. He was ready to employ every available resource to save Rangoon. He was of the view that if British took control over Burma, then their route to Delhi would not be easy and attainment of freedom will remain a dream forever.

The condition was becoming complex day by day.

There Japanese Commander-in-Chief began to vacate Rangoon. The office of Azad Hind Fauj was compulsorily shifted to Bangkok. Higher officials requested Subhash Babu to go to some safe place.

But Subhash was not ready to go anywhere. "The happiness that one gets by staying with his friends one cannot get by staying away from them. I want to stay with my soldiers in the battle field. I don't want my dear soldiers to feel inert in my absence."

But all the officers said in a singular voice, "No, you are our only source of inspiration. We need you. With the hope to see you, we can fight with the enemy. Don't endanger your life at this juncture."

After much request, Subhash left for Bangkok.

24th April 1945

Subhash Babu departed for Rangoon. As he parted with the soldiers, tears came rolling down his eyes. His heart was crying at the very thought of leaving his friends in the battle field. Addressing the soldiers and citizens who had assembled to bid fare well to him he said, "The brave soldiers and officers of Azad Hind Fauj! I am leaving you with a heavy heart. While leaving Burma I was feeling as if my heart was tearing apart. This is the place where we have fought so many battles of freedom.

Though we have faced defeat in the first phase of freedom struggle, but always remember that we have failed only in this first phase. We have to fight more and there is no reason to lose our hearts.

Friends! in this sensitive moment, I have only one word as order for you—if you have to bow before the enemy temporarily, do so like brave hearts. The future generation of India, who will be born free citizens, will sing songs in praise of your achievements.

My faith in attaining freedom is still alive. I am entrusting our national tricolor, national honor and the glorious courage of Indians in your safe hands. I have no doubts that in order to retain our country's honor, you will not hesitate to stake your lives.

My dear countrymen staying in Burma! I am sure that our emotions cannot be trampled upon. For the sake of attaining freedom I request you to retain your emotions and your pride and wait for that moment when you get an opportunity to fight for India's freedom. And when the history of India's freedom will be written, I am sure that then the Indians in Burma would be given the utmost reverence.

Today I am not leaving Burma willfully. I would have stayed back and shared the sorrow of this temporary defeat with all of you. But with the advice of my ministers and army officials and to continue with this freedom struggle, I am compelled to leave Burma. I am a born optimist. I request you all to retain this optimism.

I have always been saying that the dawn is preceded by darkness of night. We all are passing through that darkness hence do believe that the dawn is not far off. India will definitely be a free nation."

Under the supervision of Major General Loknath, 7000 soldiers stayed back in Burma.

3rd May 1945

British government captured Burma. All the soldiers of Azad Hind Fauj were made captive. Even after months of hardship they faced on the thick forests of Burma, the brave hearts of Azad Hind Fauj had to face defeat at last.

Japanese were very much scared. They were running here and there worried, but nobody was there to help them.

5th August 1945

The first atom bomb was dropped in the city of Hiroshima, and within a fraction of second Hiroshima turned into a heap of ashes. Japanese were scared and the whole world was shocked to see this holocaust.

8th August 1945

The second atom bomb was dropped in the city of Nagasaki. Now Japan had totally broken down. They did not find any reason to continue with the war. In fact they were totally shattered by such dangerous consequences of the war.

The whole world woke up to the news on 9 August 1945 that Japan had surrendered.

What else could have they done?

Many Japanese officials killed themselves for the sake of honor. Instead of facing shame at the hands of the enemy, they feel it better to embrace death.

It was really bad news. Nobody ever thought that Japan will surrender so easily. But the situation was really grave.

Subhash could not believe this sudden news. How suddenly everything happened? Curtain has fallen on this historical course of events. This was the sudden termination of Second World War.

Subhash was very much disturbed. The torch of revolution, which he had lighted, found itself in the midst of storm. The

The Inspiring Thoughts of Revolutionary Subhash

Failures

Failures are sometimes the foundation of success. Even if we fail for end numbers of times, it does not matter. It is better to fail after many attempts than never to attempt at all.

Always Move Ahead

Even though our path is full of dangers and difficulties but we have to keep marching ahead.

Ideals

In this materialistic world everything gets destroyed and will continue to do so but thoughts, ideals and dreams are indestructible. A person can die for a particular ideal but that ideal will, after that person's death, spread in the lives of thousands of people. Everything in this universe is short lived. Only one thing does not get destroying that is our ideal. Our ideal is the hope of our society. Our thoughts will never die.

Criticism

When we criticize others we should exercise control and self-perseverance. By being patient and soft we won't lose anything but will gain something more.

Hope-Despair

No power can erase the hope hidden in despair. The sweetness of life always remains in this manner.

Optimism

I am a born optimist and I will not accept defeat at any cost.

Slogan

Before dawn there is necessarily darkness. Be brave and continue with your struggle.

Worship

Whatever you want to achieve, try to get it with complete devotion and truthfulness. This is the true worship.

Duty

We only have the right to do our duty. Our duty is our responsibility.

Suffering Hardship

To attain our country's freedom as much hardships we will suffer or as much sacrifice we make, India will receive as much respect from the outside world.

Thankfulness

A person, who in spite of all his sorrows and sufferings, cries for others is sure to receive acknowledgement from others.

Revolution

Nothing great can be achieved, whether internal or external, without revolution.

Flattery

I have never indulged in flattering anybody. I don't know how to talk to appease others.

Give blood

We will be able to retain our freedom only by sacrificing our lives and blood.

Mahatma Gandhi

The work done by Mahatma Gandhi for attaining freedom for India is unparalleled and incomparable that his name will be written in history in golden words.

Character

The primary duty of a student is building up the character. Intellect, duty, everything is included in character.

Contemplation

Human being is groomed in the manner he thinks. The person who considers him weak and a sinner gradually becomes weak and a sinner. The one who considers himself pure and strong becomes pure and strong. A person achieves capabilities according to his thinking.

Worry

One who desires to touch the sky has to ignore the mountains and valleys that come in the way, in the same manner, the one who wants to fulfill his desires should not worry about any other things.

Curiosity

The way in which fragrance is necessarily associated with flowers; in the same way it is essential to have inquisitive questions in our life.

Cunningness

To me life is not so dear that I take to cunningness to survive. Physical happiness or personal success is not the basis of a successful life.

Sorrow

When I am indulged in serious thoughts I find that all the sorrows we possess have an important objective behind it. If we remember this philosophy, every moment in our life, then we won't be disturbed by worries or sorrows.

There is a feeling of innate sense of happiness even when we suffer sorrows. In the absence of such kind of happiness we would have lost of sanity. Otherwise how could we smile in the midst of sorrows?

Happiness is hidden behind our sorrows. And this is 100--true. If one does not gain happiness in his duties, then he would not be able to suffer hardships happily.

Disloyalty to the Country

If treason is not put to control in time and traitors are not meted out appropriate punishment, then no country can remain unconcerned about the safety and security of their country's freedom.

Wealth

I am not at all interested in wealth because it is the cause of all vices. In this universe only that person is wealthy in the true sense of the word, who loves God and has true devotion to Him. In comparison to such a true lover and devotee of God even big emperors are like beggars.

Fanaticism

Religious fanaticism is a thorn on the path of cultural spirituality. The only way to weed out fanaticism is to impart scientific education.

Women

As long as the Indian women do not awake, India cannot awake.

Judgement

Our judgement depends upon our assessment of views and other people.

Change

We should mould ourselves according to the need of the time.

Examination

We become impatient as we face examination. But we never think that each moment of our life is an examination. The tests we come across in our life is unending. And the results of these tests we face during our life time as well in our next births.

Impact

Whatever impact we gain in our early years of our life remains in our life for the maximum period. Whether it is good or bad, it has a deep impact on growing children's mind.

Love

The person who gives an honorable position in his heart, to anyone whom he meets on his way, imagine how large hearted that person would be and how great his love.

Sacrifice

We can attain freedom if we are ready to fight and sacrifice everything.

The time is ripe when every man, woman, girl, boy should come forward for the ultimate sacrifice to attain freedom.

If we attain freedom without sacrifice and suffering hardships, then it would be useless because then we would not be capable of keeping it safe.

Our policy should be to continue fighting for our freedom, whatever is the outcome.

Devotion and Love

If human beings make efforts he can increase his love and devotion and in this manner decrease their selfishness.

Devotional Songs

We will attain peace only when we are completely immersed in the worship of God. If peace should prevail over the earth, then each household should indulge in prayers and worship.

India

The land of India is God's favorite place. In every age God has taken birth in the form of savior on this pure land.

Indians

We should awake from our inert state. We should leave our laziness and engage ourselves in our duties. We are Indians and the welfare of India is our own welfare.

Indian Culture

I am not one among those who would forget the glory of our past in the fervor of modernism. We have to make our past our basis for the future. India has its own culture, which should be developed in its necessary directions. We have with us the assets of philosophy, literature, art and science to give to the outside world.

Emotions and Philosophy

We have to remain calm even in face of emotional outpour then only we can build our life in a constructive manner. Without emotions, philosophy is impossible.

Mind

With increasing age and experiences our mind attains more permanence.

Great men

In my opinion the importance of great men come to light with small incidents not with the big ones.

Women

I am well aware of the capabilities of Indian women. Hence I can surely say that there is no such thing that our women cannot do. And there is no sacrifice or hardships that they cannot make or face.

I want a troop of brave Indian women who form a regiment and ready for a brave death and take up the sword as Rani of Jhansi did in 1857.

Our past has been very great and bright. And if our tradition had not been so glorious, a brave woman like Rani of Jhansi would not have born in our country.

Mother

No mother could behave in a selfish manner because mother stays alive and leads the life for her children.

Human being

If every human being makes himself useful according to his strength and nature then soon life will become visible in every species.

Philanthropy

It is obvious to develop love towards those who have taken care of you. But the person, who can give respect to any person on road, is a large-hearted person and his love the greatest of all.

My ambition

As far as I am concerned, I am not perturbed or afraid of hardships. Instead of running away from them, I welcome them.

As time passes by, I all the more feel that I have a definite duty to be accomplished in my life and I am born to accomplish it.

If I have to sacrifice my comforts and embrace suffering and poverty for the sake of nation then I will heartily accept that.

My life is not for my own happiness. I am not lacking happiness in my life but it is not for materialistic pleasure because I have a mission in my life and I have my duties towards it.

If life is devoid of any struggles or dangers then the life loses its real essence.

Youth

The youth has got a new power of thinking and they will not follow anything blindly. They have realized that they are the heir apparent to the future and they have to free India at any cost.

Nation

If a country loses its life-power and its internal liveliness then it has no right to survive anymore.

National Freedom

The kind of freedom we are expecting, that can never be achieved without paying the price of sacrifice and suffering of hardship. Those of us who have the heart to experience this and want to take this opportunity, should come forward with the flowers of worship.

National Upgradation

The foundation of nation's development can only be said on the earth of sacrifice and suffering.

Money

Those who earn money should have the feeling in their heart, that – 'Money is soil and soil is money' (Rupiya Mitti, Mitti Rupaiya). One who has this feeling will never become selfish or spendthrift.

Thought

The thoughts that, during youth, try to chart out a course (path) in the midst of oppositions and obstructions grow up to be serious as one becomes mature.

The thought that takes birth straightaway in our heart, they are more capable as compared to others whether it expressed in a layman's language or an ornamental one and the other thoughts are expressed ornamentally.

Students

Our duty should be to instill the feeling of unity in the minds of students so that through them the people of India remain united throughout.

Every student should possess a healthy and strong physique, strong characters, necessary information and a brain full of healthy and mobile thoughts. Your life is your own and the responsibility of developing it lies with you than anyone else.

School

I despise some Indians, who, on the lives of English public schools, are desirous of running Indian schools with British teachers.

Triumph

Triumph of the child is the triumph of the mother and the defeat of the child, the mother's defeat.

Worship of Brave Hearts

Those who want to become great personalities should begin their life by worshipping greatness and great men. Those who want to become a brave heart should learn to worship heroes.

Strength

Without facing tests no person can assess in a definitive manner, how much strength he possesses.

Teacher

If the teacher is not competent, then primary education can never be successful. A teacher should possess the qualities of love and sympathy in his heart. A teacher should be able to look at things in the perspective of his/her students.

Education

It is very essential as well as profitable to impart education through the medium of stories. In this manner children will not feel that they are learning to read & write.

The objective of education is to hone the intellect and develop correct thinking. If both these objectives are achieved then it means that the aim of education has been fulfilled.

Devotion

I need only devotion. With devotion the religious feeling gets awakened and in turn I gain knowledge. Great saints have said that devotion leads to the path of knowledge gaining.

Lack of devotion is the root of all misfortunes and sorrows.

Music

In my opinion one that lacks the beat of music in his heart, he can never be a great person.

Patience

Undoubtedly in the childhood years as well as during youth days one should be pure and exercise patience.

True Revolutionary

A true revolutionary never accepts defeat. He never loses hope. A true revolutionary has full faith in the necessity of his objective and will ensure that his objective gets fulfilled at the end.

Madness

A person who is not mad can never become a great person. But every mad person cannot be great or skilful.

Honor

I value life very much but I love honor much more than life.

Sacrifice everything

As an Indian I have always been fighting for attaining India's freedom. I expect that, all Indians, wherever they are, should sacrifice everything for the sake of freeing India from foreign clutches.

Happiness & Peace

If we are not experiencing happiness and peace at heart, then one can never be happy in the true sense.

Army

The army which is not traditionally courageous, brave or invincible cannot win over a strong and powerful enemy.

Service

True service is to give away the most valuable thing in you possession.

My prayer to God is to spend my whole life in helping others.

If we think about ourselves and lead a life free of moral values like animals, then what is the meaningfulness of taking birth as human being? Only that life is worth living which is dedicated for the service of others.

Soldier

Being a soldier you have to stick to the three ideals of dedication, duty and sacrifice. The soldier who is a patriot and is ready to lay down his life are invincible.

Army Strength

The World War has shown us that the country that does not possess army strength cannot retain its independence.

Independence

The independence attained without bloodshed is not a real freedom.

Swarajya

As long as the people of India together do not face the enemy till then it is not easy to attain freedom and even if freedom is attained it is difficult to safeguard it.

Health

Ignoring one's own health is not only an offense against oneself but also to others and towards the nation.

Himalaya

If there is something invaluable or glorious in India those memories are associated with Himalayas.